ANSWERING ORTHODOXY

A Catholic Response to Attacks from the East

MICHAEL LOFTON

Catholic
Answers
Press

Published by Catholic Answers, Inc.
2020 Gillespie Way
El Cajon, California 92020
1-888-291-8000 orders
619-387-0042 fax
catholic.com

Printed in the United States of America

Cover design by ebooklaunch.com
Interior design by Russell Graphic Design

978-1-68357-334-0
978-1-68357-335-7 Kindle
978-1-68357-336-4 ePub

Dedicated to His Holiness Pope Francis and
His All-Holiness the Ecumenical Patriarch Bartholomew I

For the restoration of all unity!

*He who states his case first seems right,
until the other comes and examines him.*

—Proverbs 18:17

*Diverse weights and diverse measures are both alike an
abomination to the LORD.*

—Proverbs 20:10

*We accept and approve all the letters of the blessed Pope Leo that
he composed on the subject of the Christian religion. Whence, as
we have said, following the Apostolic See [Rome] in all matters
and proclaiming all that has been determined by it, I hope that
I may deserve to be in the one communion with you that the
Apostolic See proclaims, in which there is the complete and true
solidity of the Christian religion: we promise also that the names
of those who are separated from the communion of the Catholic
Church, that is, who are not in agreement with the Apostolic See,
will not be recited in the sacred mysteries. Moreover, I have signed
this profession of my faith with my own hand and have offered it
to you, Hormisdas, holy and venerable pope of the city of Rome.*

—*Libellus fidei* of Pope Hormisdas, August 11, 515

Contents

PART 2
HISTORICAL ATTACKS

PART 3
LITURGICAL ATTACKS

Preface

I still remember feeling betrayed by the Catholic Church.

I became a Catholic in 2012 because I was convinced that the Church checked out on paper. I was able to see the biblical, historical, and rational reasons for its claims. However, I soon began to notice a wide chasm between the Catholic Church as described in theory and the Church as seen in action. I came to call it a conflict between "paper Catholicism" and "experiential Catholicism." The cognitive dissonance from this tension severely tested my faith for several years.

Concerns about my conversion to Catholicism amassed, but I remained faithful to my reception into the Church. With the use of Catholic apologetics, I even defended the Church from opposing family members and friends. However, it wasn't long before this fidelity to the Church was tried even more, especially as I began to realize that I was surrounded by both clergy and laity who did not believe what the Catholic Church teaches in many areas. To make matters worse, my experiences of evil treatment by Catholic clergy, and betrayal from Catholic friends, rubbed salt in the wounds, and I struggled to find a good spiritual director to guide me through the torment of a scrupulous conscience.

It all came to a head when a local priest gave incredibly injurious and spiritually destructive advice to someone close to me, with disastrous consequences for me and my children.

This was the straw that broke the camel's back. I felt betrayed by the same Church I had defended for over five years.

At this point, I began to wonder if God had allowed me to go through all of this in order to point me to Eastern Orthodoxy. I had considered Orthodoxy for several years before becoming a Catholic. So I re-evaluated Eastern Orthodoxy over the course of the next two years—and then I took the plunge.

From an experiential perspective, my time in Orthodoxy was incredible. I had the exact opposite experience with my priest and local congregation of what I had had with the Catholic Church. However, problems of a different nature arose—namely, theological and practical issues. In other words, I found "experiential Orthodoxy" soothing, but "paper Orthodoxy" did not make sense.

This problem—the result of the Eastern Orthodox lacking an objective and final teaching authority—certainly concerned me, but the biggest issue I experienced was a conviction that I shouldn't have broken communion with the Catholic Church because of personal problems. Did I have doctrinal, historical, and liturgical reasons to go to Eastern Orthodoxy? Yes, but these arose after I had already arrived at a point of dissatisfaction with Catholicism. In the midst of it all, the words of the Second Vatican Council rang in my ears:

> Hence they could not be saved who, knowing that the Catholic Church was founded as necessary by God through Christ, would refuse either to enter it, or to remain in it (*Lumen Gentium* 14).

These words pierced my heart daily and forced me to question whether I had made the right decision. Having had time and distance from the emotional situations that caused me to be disillusioned with the Catholic Church, I was able to consider the claims for Catholicism and the claims for Orthodoxy in a more objective fashion.

After three additional years of study and discernment, I returned to communion with the Catholic Church out of conviction that I must remain there if I wish to be saved, as the Second Vatican Council states.

I am grateful for my time in Orthodoxy, as it taught me the beauty of the Jesus Prayer, how to live as an Eastern Christian, and how to relate to disillusioned Catholics who look to the Orthodox for greener pastures. This book is partly the fruit of that experience.

Those who may be tempted, as I once was, by Eastern Orthodoxy may buy in to common Orthodox objections to Catholicism without sufficiently evaluating them. Therefore, the primary purpose of this book is to help disillusioned Catholics work through common Orthodox objections to Catholic doctrine and communion, many of which I had to work through in order to return to the Catholic Church. By engaging these objections, I hope to urge disillusioned Catholics to re-examine their decision to look elsewhere, since the doctrinal basis the Orthodox use to justify their separation with Rome is without merit.

In addition, this book will be useful for Eastern Orthodox who have objections to Catholicism and wish to know the Catholic response. More importantly, it will help them realize that there are no sufficient grounds for their separation from Catholic communion.

Finally, Protestants, who often share objections against Catholicism with the Eastern Orthodox, will benefit from this book in multiple ways. First, it will show them that the Catholic position has a robust defense against their objections.

Second, for those who are interested in converting to an apostolic church, it will help them in their discernment between the Catholic Church and the Eastern Orthodox churches.

I've arranged this work into four parts. The first offers a brief history of the division between the Catholic Church and the Eastern Orthodox churches. Though it is certainly not an exhaustive survey, it will be an adequate overview of the many tensions that led to the division. The next part deals with doctrinal objections leveled by Eastern Orthodox against the Catholic Church. After this, I offer various historical objections against the Church that a Catholic will encounter if he begins discerning Eastern Orthodoxy. Finally, I offer several liturgical objections commonly cited by Orthodox against Catholics. The objections in this last section are more trivial but also much more prevalent. Where helpful, in some chapters, I will also provide brief summaries of Orthodox belief on questions of theology or doctrine, the better to inform the reader of where the Orthodox are coming from when they make their objections against the Catholic position.

Having offered responses to each of the objections in these three categories, I hope to sufficiently demonstrate that there are good responses available to those who are truly willing to consider the Catholic position in this debate.

Monroe, Louisiana
On the Sunday of the Fathers
of the Seventh Ecumenical Council, 2022

The History of the Catholic and Orthodox Divide

When my parents divorced, I had to choose between them—but it's not what you think! Please afford me the chance to explain before you jump to conclusions.

Many years ago, my father and mother were married and deeply loved each other. But over time, difficulties arose between them, which caused a slow deterioration in the health of their relationship and, eventually and regrettably, divorce. And worse, their separation had the unintended result of dividing my brother and me from each other, as each of us chose a different parent to live with.

My brother and I now have two different lives with very different backgrounds, each stemming from the parent each of us chose. You'll probably agree that children shouldn't have to make such decisions because of the failures of their parents.

Now, you may think I'm talking about my biological father, mother, and brother. And maybe I was—but I'm *also* referring to my spiritual father, the Catholic Church; my spiritual mother, the Eastern Orthodox churches; and my spiritual brother, my Orthodox lay brethren. As a Catholic who has been Eastern Orthodox, both of my spiritual parents are responsible for who I am today. As such, I deeply desire to see unity between my parents. I have even dedicated my life to it.

Before there can be healing and unity between Catholics and Orthodox, we must examine what led to the separation, much like a couple who wish to restore their relationship. After all, if the cause of a medical disease is not discerned, it is unlikely that the proper remedy will be provided. So it is with the Catholic and Orthodox divide.

Examining this history will also help Catholics, Orthodox, and Protestants to be more familiar with how we ended up in the state of separation we are in today. Familiarity with this will help them further determine that the schism was unjustified and should not be perpetuated by their actions.*

Sadly, when surveying the relations between Catholic West and Orthodox East, we quickly observe a long and drawn-out history of friction and deterioration. In the same way a divorce can be the result of a long and subtle breakdown in communication and relations between a husband and wife, so too it is with the Catholic and Orthodox divide.

We start to see tremors of this division as early as the second century, where Pope St. Victor I (189-199) threatened to excommunicate the churches of Asia minor over a dispute about the proper date of Easter. Some claimed they had a tradition from the apostles that Easter should be on the fourteenth of the ancient Jewish month of Nisan, whereas others claimed that it should be on whatever Sunday fell after the fourteenth of Nisan. This was patched up after several figures, including St. Irenaeus, engaged in some skillful East-West diplomacy.

Sadly, there were many other divisions to come after this event.

---

*   A full treatment of the division between East and West may be found in the Protestant historian Henry Chadwick's work *East and West: The Making of a Rift in the Church*.

The fourth century saw an incredible amount of ecclesiastical turmoil and confusion. Though Nicene Christology was successfully defended and codified at the Council of Nicaea (325), this success was immediately met with resistance from many bishops in the East, who either outright rejected it or wished to adopt a modified version. This put much of the East in opposition with the bishop of Rome, along with St. Athanasius. But by the end of the fourth century, orthodoxy triumphed, and there was peace between much of the East and the West—though this too would be short lived.

In the fifth century, Christological debates in the East about the personhood and natures of Jesus led to several divisions that last to this day. For instance, the Assyrian Church of the East broke communion with the Catholic Church, the Eastern Orthodox churches, and the Oriental Orthodox churches when it rejected the Council of Ephesus (431). The Oriental Orthodox broke away from the Catholic Church and the Eastern Orthodox Churches with its rejection of the Council of Chalcedon (451) and Constantinople II (553). It may be argued that most, if not all, of these divisions were the result of a breakdown in language and political disputes more than doctrinal differences. However, the net result of several formal divisions remains.

The fifth century saw further tremors between East and West when the patriarch of Constantinople (an important Eastern bishop over the new capital of the Roman Empire), in an attempt to win back those who had rejected the Council of Chalcedon, failed to fully uphold Chalcedon. This led to Constantinople, and those in the East who supported it, finding themselves out of communion with Rome for over four decades, in what has come to be known as the *Acacian Schism*. This was patched up by Pope Hormisdas, whose formula or *libellus* 250 Eastern bishops were required to sign to be restored to communion with the Catholic Church.

The sixth century had some bumps in the road, too. The Byzantine emperor, the leader of the Eastern half of the Roman Empire, made some unsavory moves against the pope in an attempt to heal the division with those who had rejected the Council of Chalcedon. In the year 553, he held the fifth ecumenical council and attempted to force the pope's participation and approbation. When things did not go according to plan, the council attempted to suspend the pope. Eventually, the pope and the emperor came to an agreement, but the situation left relations between East and West strained.

In the seventh century, there arose another heresy over whether Christ has one or two wills. Some in the East, backed by the emperor, asserted that Christ has only one will in order to accommodate those who were dissatisfied with Chalcedon's emphasis on the two natures of Christ. This new heresy, called *Monothelitism*, offended a few bishops in the East, but especially the pope in the West. The true doctrine of two wills in Christ prevailed at the sixth ecumenical council (680-681), which was called to reassert the pope's position, though it mistakenly condemned a previous pope, Honorius, for himself allegedly holding to Monothelitism.

The council's adoption of Rome's *dyothelite* (two wills in Christ) position resolved the brief rupture between Rome and many in the East. Yet, in the next year, the Council of Trullo (691-692) stirred up petty disputes with the West over disciplinary differences, such as priestly celibacy. At the time, the differences were not enough to break ties between East and West—but some of them would find their way into later polemical works.

In the eighth century, Byzantine *iconoclasm* damaged relations with the West. The Byzantine emperor's encroachment on missionary territory belonging to the pope did not help. In the end, the papacy triumphantly defended iconography in the East with the Second Council of Nicaea (787)—and yet the tension between East and West remained.

It should be noted that up until the eighth century, the East had spent a considerable amount of time outside communion with Rome. Orthodox scholar Fr. Alexander Schmemann (1921-1983) appeals to the historian Louis Duchesne (1843-1922) to confirm this claim:

> According to Duchesne's calculation, in the period from Constantine to the seventh ecumenical council, the Eastern Church was in schism with Rome for 203 years in all; but dogmatic problems and heresies—never the rejection of the papacy—were always the cause of the break.[1]

This should be considered carefully, as it shows that the East was prone to heterodoxy in the first millennium. Up until this time, the heresies of the East were mostly about Christological matters rather than disputes over the papacy. However, this would change in the ninth century.

The ninth century saw many disputes between the pope and the patriarch of Constantinople. Much of this centered on a highly intelligent, though controversial, claimant to the throne of Constantinople, Photius (810-893), whose disputed claim to the see caused a stir with Rome. Photius's rash attempt to condemn the *filioque*,* his spurning of various Western disciplinary practices, and—most imprudently—his attempt to excommunicate the pope resulted in a deep mistrust in the West.

Photius was initially condemned but eventually restored to communion with Rome. However, his rash attempt at judging

---

*   For more on the *filioque*, see Objection 4.

the Roman See and his treatise against the *filioque* (which he misunderstood) would be echoed in later polemics against Rome. Toward the end of this century, relations between East and West were restored, but they hung by a thread.

It was in the eleventh century that many of the underlying tensions from previous centuries came to a swelling point. Constantinople dropped Rome from the diptychs (a list of those alive and dead whom the Church commemorates), which meant they no longer recognized the pope as being in communion.

Inquiries made into the matter showed that this was simply a reality, rooted in fact more than any canonical decision. When Pope Leo IX (1049-1054) sent Cardinal Humbert (1000-1061) to Constantinople in 1054 to resolve the dispute, tempers were lost, theological polemics were exchanged, and eventually the cardinal and patriarch excommunicated each other. This was not a moment where all of the Eastern churches severed ties with Rome, though it is often portrayed that way in popular circles, but it certainly impaired relations with the West.

In the late twelfth century, Constantinople massacred its Latin Catholic inhabitants for political reasons. Twenty-two years later, at the turn of the thirteenth century, a crusader army made up of Venetian Catholics sacked Constantinople in a dispute over promised payments, in what is known as the Fourth Crusade. Though the pope forbade this act, and had already excommunicated the Venetians involved, the papacy took advantage of the conquered city by acknowledging the newly installed Latin patriarch there. Having a rival Latin patriarch over the same jurisdiction claimed by the Greek patriarch of Constantinople poured acid in the wounds of Eastern Christians, who were shocked by the actions of their Western brethren. Relations with the East further deteriorated after this.

An attempt was made to restore communion between Rome and Constantinople in the late thirteenth century at the Second Council of Lyon (1272-1274), but this was largely an agreement between the pope and the emperor. Not enough clergy and laity were on board, so the reunion was superficial, and the Orthodox almost immediately rejected it.

In the fifteenth century, the East experienced significant losses in territory at the hands of the Turks. This put serious pressure on the emperor to work toward reconciliation with the pope, whose aid the East could use. Thus, the Orthodox churches met with the pope at the Council of Florence (1438-1445) in an attempt to hash out their theological differences. This led to most of the Eastern bishops signing off on the papal claims and agreeing to the Church's formulations on other disputed topics, like the *filioque* and purgatory. Tragically, the Orthodox bishops who signed the agreement almost immediately repudiated it, especially because their laity rejected the council.

After the Orthodox's repudiation of the reunion council, the schism between East and West was almost entirely sealed. Occasional instances of sharing in each other's sacraments occurred, but by the mid-eighteenth century, even this effectively ceased when it was discovered that several patriarchs of Antioch had secretly converted to Catholicism.

It is noteworthy that reunion efforts from Florence onward were not entirely fruitless. Most of what we now call the Eastern Catholic churches came into communion with Rome, through separate agreements, from the period of the Council of Florence unto recent times. These were reunions with particular churches from parts of Eastern Orthodoxy, Oriental Orthodoxy, and the Assyrian Church of the East. In a real sense, many of these reunions were efforts to heal the schisms that began in the fifth century. However, some, especially those remaining Eastern Orthodox, have looked on these efforts as acts of betrayal by the Eastern Catholics and further occasions for mistrust in Rome.

Having reviewed some of the reasons that led to the schism between Catholics and Eastern Orthodox, it is clear that naming an exact date when "the schism" occurred—let alone defining one single schism!—is a tall order, and probably impossible. What can be said confidently is that the schism between the Catholic Church and the Eastern Orthodox churches began brewing in the second century and truly came to a head after the Orthodox formally repudiated the reunion of the Council of Florence.

PART 1

DOCTRINAL ATTACKS

At the end of the day, it doesn't matter so much when the schism occurred, who started it, and why. At their heart, the issues between Eastern Orthodox and Catholics are issues of doctrine (teachings), and all of them can be either resolved or shown to be immaterial to the Eastern Orthodox reuniting with Rome.

However, in Christianity there is a strong need to preserve the teachings that have been handed down from Jesus and the apostles, since these teachings are given to the church for its spiritual growth. To depart from a teaching of Jesus—or worse, to contradict it—is something that Christians wish to avoid in order to be faithful followers of Jesus. Consequently, doctrinal disputes between Catholics and Orthodox are seen as serious because a church that holds to a false teaching is promoting a way that corrupts or opposes

Jesus' teachings. For this reason, an examination of the most common doctrinal objections leveled by Eastern Orthodox against Catholicism is in order.

1

"Jesus is the head of the Church, not the pope"

Most Orthodox claim that Jesus is the head of the Church and that no single bishop can be called its head. However, a small minority are willing to concede that the pope (the bishop of Rome), under certain conditions, may be called the head of the Church—but only in a very qualified way.

Catholics tend to emphasize that Jesus is the invisible and heavenly head who reigns supreme over the Church and that the pope is the visible and earthly head, who is subservient to Jesus.

What do Eastern Orthodox believe about the pope? Unfortunately, there isn't one unified view on the papacy, since the Orthodox have not definitively weighed in on the matter. However, a common view is that he is the first among equals, which itself may be understood differently among the Orthodox. That being said, there is general agreement among the Orthodox that the first among equals does not mean that the bishop who is the first has the ability to impose himself in the affairs of another bishop's territory. As first among equals, he may be given the highest honor in the Church, and his words may be respected, but he is not able to exercise any binding authority outside his jurisdiction—unless he has the consent of the rest of the bishops. Consequently, the Orthodox object to some of the titles Catholics give to the pope, such as "head of the Church." Additionally, Orthodox would claim that the first among equals title is not necessarily something that Jesus has bestowed on any particular bishop—but is something the post-apostolic bishops have bestowed on the most prominent bishop among them.

A Catholic who encounters Orthodox apologists (someone who defends the Church's claims) will often hear: "Jesus is the head of the Church, not the pope!" In fact, these were the words of an Orthodox priest who emphatically tried to dissuade me from returning to Catholic communion. This is certainly not a new objection, unique to this priest. In fact, it has a long history in Orthodox polemics against Catholicism, going back to the letter of an unnamed thirteenth-century patriarch of Constantinople to a patriarch of Jerusalem.[2] When disillusioned Catholics begin to discern converting to Eastern Orthodoxy, they are immediately confronted by this claim, and they often find it convincing without thinking it through.

I must admit, I was not impressed by this objection when I first heard it. After all, how could Catholics be accused of putting the pope "at the top" when every Catholic must confess that Jesus is the head of the Catholic Church? This is evident from numerous scriptural passages—e.g., 1 Corinthians 11:3, along with Ephesians 1:22 and 5:23—and is wholeheartedly admitted by Catholics, who hold to these verses as inspired by God. So the question is not whether Jesus is the head of the Church—he is!—but whether it is legitimate to make a distinction between an invisible and visible head of the Church.

Before answering this question, it may be helpful to define what we mean by *church*. The term *church* (from the

Greek *ekklēsia*) most natively refers to a local assembly of Christians gathered around a bishop in a particular territory. The term may also refer to the fellowship of all local churches who recognize one another in faith, worship, and governance. In other words, the term may be considered on a universal level as well as a local one.

Returning to the question, in his polemical work defending the teachings of the Eastern Orthodox churches, the Orthodox priest Fr. Michael Azkoul argues that it is heretical to say the pope is the visible head of the Church. In a footnote defining the term *papism*, Azkoul argues,

> "Papism" (from the Greek *papas* = father) is a word often used to describe Roman Catholicism; it refers specifically to the heresy of elevating one bishop to be visible head of the universal Church.[3]

We have to wonder how consistent Orthodox like Fr. Azkoul, and others who share his objection, would be if they applied this objection to their own ecclesiology (the study of how the Church is structured and functions). For example, Eastern Orthodox generally have no problem speaking of a local bishop as the head of a eucharistic assembly in his own territory. For instance, the eminent Orthodox scholar Fr. John Meyendorff (1926-1992), building on the work of St. Ignatius of Antioch (108-140), says of the local bishop,

> He is not only a "symbol" of Christ. Through him the presence of the body is real in the community. "I beseech you," writes Ignatius of Antioch about the year 100, "seek to do all things in divine harmony, *under the presidency of the bishop, who has the place of God at your meeting*" (Magn. VI).[4]

In other words, Meyendorff sees the bishop in his territory as the visible manifestation of the invisible God. Yet who would say that Jesus is not the head of the eucharistic assembly because the local bishop is the head? If the distinction between a visible and invisible head is afforded to the Orthodox on the local level of a bishop's eparchy—i.e., his diocese—then the distinction is at least potentially legitimate for Catholics who see the pope as the head of the universal Church. What is good for the goose is good for the gander.

Moreover, this distinction can be seen between Jesus and the apostles, who were all considered heads, but in different ways. Pope St. Gregory the Great (540-604) notes,

> Certainly Peter, the first of the apostles, himself a member of the holy and universal Church, Paul, Andrew, John—what were they but heads of particular communities? And yet all were members under one head.[5]

Clearly, there was one sense in which the apostles were all heads of churches, but another sense in which Jesus was the head of them all! So, to refer to someone as the head does not automatically detract from Christ's headship.

Another example is Ephesians 5:23, which calls the husband the "head of the wife" in the same way that Jesus is the "head of the Church." Yet who in his right mind would say the headship of the husband is in opposition to the headship of Christ over all humans, including wives? Likewise, the headship of the pope over the Church is not in opposition to the headship of Christ over his body.

At this juncture, the only question that remains is whether such a distinction may be appropriately applied to the pope in the context of the universal Church. To answer this question, an appeal may be made to common ground between Catholics and Orthodox—namely, the ecumenical councils.

According to the Orthodox theologian Fr. Michael Pomazansky (1888-1988), the ecumenical councils rejected the claim that the bishop of Rome is the head of the churches.[6] But is this true? Consider the Council of Chalcedon (451), where the papal legate (representative) Paschasinus describes the pope in the presence of the bishops of the council as "the most blessed and apostolic bishop of the city of Rome, the head of all the churches."[7] This is done with no protest by the Eastern bishops present at the council. Pomazansky overlooks this instance.

Additionally, it is worth noting that according to Fr. Michael Azkoul's words above, this statement from Paschasinus should be considered heretical. And yet, an ecumenical council did not protest against it.

Paschasinus's statement is not the only one of its kind. A few centuries later, the Palestinian bishop Stephen of Dor presented himself to Pope Martin I (649-655) at the Lateran Synod of 649 and asserted that the pope "presides over all others" on the basis of Rome's apostolic roots in St. Peter, who was given the keys of the kingdom.[8] Interestingly, Orthodox Edward Siecienski expressly states that Rome's authority was proclaimed in this synod and cites the words of Stephen of Dor. Interacting with the comments of the scholars Fr. Richard Price and Phil Booth, who translated the synod into English, he says,

> At the synod Rome's orthodoxy and authority were boldly trumpeted by all, Stephen of Dora calling it "the supreme and sovereign See . . . that rules and presides over all the others." For Stephen Rome's authority was solidly grounded in "the truly great Peter, the head of the apostles, [who]

was deemed worthy not only to be entrusted, alone out of all, with the 'keys of the kingdom of heaven' . . . but also because he was the first to be entrusted with shepherding the sheep of the whole Catholic Church."[9]

Amazingly, an Eastern Orthodox scholar admits that an Eastern bishop at this synod believed that the pope is the head of the Church! This demonstrates that the concept of the pope as head of the other churches was alive in the East in the millennia when the first seven ecumenical councils were occurring.

Another interesting passage related to this subject comes up in Pope Hadrian (772-795)'s letter to Patriarch Tarasios of Constantinople (730-806), which was read out loud before the council fathers of the Second Council of Nicaea (787). Curiously, in this letter, the pope calls the Apostolic See of Rome "the head of all the churches of God."[10] As noted above, this was certainly not new to Byzantine ears due to the relatively recently concluded Council of Ephesus, but also because the emperor Justinian (482-565) had already spoken of the pope as the "head of all the churches."[11] Yet, instead of the patriarch of Constantinople and the council fathers contesting these claims, Tarasios and the fathers explicitly said of Hadrian's letters, "We follow, accept, and approve them."[12]

Orthodox presbyter Fr. Laurent A. Cleenewerck, read Pope Hadrian's claims as asserting headship over the universal Church. Cleenewerck comments on Hadrian, saying,

Since the times of [Pope] Stephen, the Roman church has consistently taught that her bishop is the successor of Peter in a unique sense and that he holds by divine right a primacy of power over the universal Church. In other words, Rome made no secret that her ecclesiology and concept of primacy were different from that of the East, as we have seen in the reaction of Pope Leo to the canons of Chalcedon. This was expressed consistently and unambiguously by a number of popes commemorated as saints in the Orthodox Church, including such luminaries as Leo, Agatho, and Hadrian. . . . This ecclesiology was accepted by a number of Eastern saints.[13]

In summary, Orthodox ecclesiology allows for the visible-invisible distinction to be employed in its own ecclesiology, so to portray Catholics as pitting the headship of Christ against the headship of the pope is to use unequal weights in criticism of the Catholic position. This is why Orthodox priest and author Fr. John Panteleimon Manoussakis scolds Orthodox who use this argument against Catholics:

> Another position that one hears often from the Orthodox is that the Church needs no *primus* because Christ himself is the head of the Church. But is this true exclusively on the universal level? Indeed, on both the regional and local levels, ecclesial structures presuppose that the bishop is Christ's living icon. No Orthodox would accept the claim that the bishop is not needed as head of either the diocese or the metropolitanate simply because that role is filled by Christ himself. Furthermore, such a naïve assertion ignores the profound theological significance of Christ's ascension and runs the risk of degenerating into some individualist, private piety that would dispense with the ecclesial structure altogether.[14]

He even calls this view, expressed by some Orthodox, heretical:

The phenomenon of anti-papism, understood as the denial of a *primus* for the universal Church and the elevation of such denial to a trait that allegedly identifies the whole Orthodox Church, is, properly speaking, heretical.[15]

In other words, Orthodox are wrong to claim that it is heretical to say the pope is head of all the churches—and in saying so, they might be guilty of heresy themselves! Moreover, we could add that the denial that the pope is head of the universal Church goes against the belief of the same council fathers that the Orthodox hold in the highest esteem. Thus, when Catholics discerning Eastern Orthodoxy encounter this objection from the Orthodox, they should ask whether the person making the objection is being consistent.

Perhaps it would be best to conclude this objection with the words of the Orthodox scholar Fr. Alexander Schmemann:

If the Church is a universal organism, she must have at her head a universal bishop as the focus of her unity and the organ of supreme power. The idea, popular in Orthodox apologetics, that the Church can have no visible head, because Christ is her *invisible* head, is theological nonsense. If applied consistently, it should also eliminate the necessity for the visible head of each local church, i.e., the bishop.[16]

2

"Papal infallibility makes ecumenical councils obsolete"

Almost all Orthodox across the board reject the claim that the pope is infallible (protected from error) in matters of faith and morals. Some Orthodox believe that the ecumenical councils can teach infallibly on matters of faith and morals, whereas other Orthodox say their teachings are infallible only if all of the Orthodox recognize them as such.

The Catholic Church maintains that the pope can teach infallibly on matters of faith and morals—under very limited conditions. It holds that ecumenical councils may also teach infallibly on faith and morals under certain conditions.

When some Catholics encounter the argument that papal infallibility makes ecumenical councils obsolete, they may become alarmed. After all, why bother having an ecumenical council weigh in on a matter if the pope is infallible? In other words, why has the Catholic Church bothered to hold twenty-one ecumenical councils if the pope could simply grab his pen and settle all theological disputes in one fell swoop?

This question is certainly worth answering, as it appears to have some merit on the surface. But first, let's see the objection from the Eastern Orthodox priest and author, Fr. Andrew Damick, who summarizes it as follows:

> An infallible pope . . . makes councils deciding doctrinal questions unnecessary, yet Christian history is filled with councils. Rather than go to all the expense of transporting hundreds of bishops and using up months and sometimes years of their time, why did they not just write to the pope to ask him to decide the question? These many councils (which fill even the history of Roman Catholicism) often speak boldly without any sense that they are mere advisers to the pope.[17]

Aside from the fact that Catholics don't claim that the bishops are "mere advisers" to the pope, the doctrine of papal infallibility is quite often misunderstood by Orthodox. Some think papal infallibility makes other organs of teaching authority in the Church, such as the bishops gathered in ecumenical councils, useless or superfluous. In fairness to Orthodox, this misunderstanding was once shared by some Catholics and Protestants, who thought the era of councils was obsolete after papal infallibility was defined in 1870.[18] So when an Orthodox defender raises this objection, some sympathy can be admitted.

The problem here is that the objection approaches the question of papal infallibility and ecumenical councils from a practical perspective when it should instead consider it from the viewpoint of objective doctrine. After all, if Christ instituted two distinctly infallible organs for the Church's teaching authority—namely, the pope and the college of bishops—then the objection loses its force. We can consider the doctrinal claims—and will, later on in this book—but for now, it is worth entertaining the practical objection.

The issue here seems to be the premise that one infallible organ in the Church would make another infallible organ obsolete. But consider how infallibility is treated in the Old Testament. For example, 2 Peter 1:21 notes that the Old Testament prophets were "moved by the Holy Spirit," and they "spoke from God." Given that God is infallible, he would not inspire his prophets to prophesy falsely. In fact, Deuteronomy 18:22 explicitly states that a failed prophecy is the telltale sign of a false prophet.

Yet we also read in the Old Testament that the Urim and the Thummim—two items used by the high priest of Israel—were used to infallibly determine knowledge from God. For instance, in 1 Samuel 14:24–47, the Urim and the Thummim are used to reliably identify who had broken King Saul's command.

Thus, there were at least two ways God could infallibly speak to the Israelites, yet non-Catholic Christians would not say that one made the other obsolete. Similarly, there were moments in history where more than one apostle was alive, and nobody would say one apostle's infallibility, active when writing Sacred Scripture, would make the infallibility of another apostle redundant.

In the New Testament, we find other ways in which God could make known his infallible will. For one, he could speak through an apostle under divine inspiration, as noted above. Simultaneously, he could reveal his will through the casting of lots, which the apostles did in Acts 1:23–26 when they needed to determine a successor to the apostle Judas. So, once again, a Christian already has precedents for multiple means of infallibility, which would not make any particular method obsolete.

Now to the other objection raised by Fr. Damick above: Why didn't the saints simply write to the pope to settle matters of dispute instead of going through the trouble of holding an ecumenical council?

A skeptic could turn this argument back around on an Orthodox and ask why the children of Israel consulted prophets when they could have simply consulted the Urim and the Thummim, or vice versa. But of course, there *were* occasions when people did write to the pope to settle a matter of dispute instead of calling for an ecumenical council! For instance, St. Cyril of Alexandria (376-444) wrote to Pope Celestine (422-432) requesting his decision on the orthodoxy of the patriarch of Constantinople, Nestorius (386-451). He states,

> We shall not publicly withdraw from communion with him until we have shared this matter with your religiousness. Therefore be so good as to decree what you think right, and whether one ought to be in communion with him or rather issue a public refusal on the grounds that no one can be in communion with one who holds and teaches such things. The policy of your perfection should be published in letters to the most devout and most God-beloved bishops of Macedonia and to all those in the East.[19]

In the same letter, Cyril has already personally judged Nestorius as heterodox, but he wants a definitive judgment from the pope to know whether he made the right choice or if he should remain in communion with Nestorius. He also notes that the decision of the pope should be published and promulgated as authoritative in all of the East. Why would Cyril do this if he did not believe that the pope could offer a definitive judgment on the case?

Some might further ask, why, then, did Celestine agree to hold the Council of Ephesus (431)? What need was there for an ecumenical council if the pope could just judge the matter himself? A brief examination of Pope St. Leo the Great, a saint in the Catholic Church and in the Eastern Orthodox churches, may provide an answer.

Prior to the Council of Chalcedon (451)—that is, the fourth ecumenical council—Leo wrote a lengthy letter to Flavian of Constantinople (d. 449), known as the *Tome of Leo*, that settled various Christological issues. It is certainly the case that Leo believed that his *Tome* was a definitive doctrinal judgment, even before the Council of Chalcedon considered it. The Catholic translator and historian Fr. Richard Price confirms this, saying,

> Before the Council of Chalcedon, Pope Leo had claimed that an ecumenical council to discuss the Faith was uncalled for since his own Tome had settled the question at issue.[20]

However, Leo also permitted these Christological questions to be confirmed by an ecumenical council in order that, "by a fuller judgment," error might be abolished.[21]

Why would something that has already been definitely judged need a "fuller judgment"? To answer this question, a helpful distinction between the formal authority and the material authority of the Church is in order. Catholic scholar Lawrence Jerome King explains this distinction:

> With regard to formal authority, a pope and a council may be equal. But as the Church is a human institution in addition to being a divine institution, the effectiveness of its teachers "does not rest solely on the authority of their office," but also on human factors. And on this material level, a council has many advantages that a pope does not: it has access to the wisdom of more individuals, [and] it

has a representative character and is therefore more easily accepted as authoritative by the people of the Church.[22]

In other words, papal infallibility is certainly sufficient to settle a doctrinal dispute, but it may not always be the most effective way, since it may not have the most visible character of universal representation. For this reason, a "fuller judgment" may be more prudent when settling certain disputes.

It is for the purpose of a "fuller judgment" that Leo allowed an ecumenical council to weigh in on the Christological matters he had settled. The same may be said for Pope Celestine and the Council of Ephesus. One may even say the same for Constantinople III (680-681), as even Orthodox scholar Edward Siecienski admits that Pope Agatho (678-681) merely expected the council to accept his definitive judgment on the case of Dyothelitism, which itself was a repetition of the definitive judgment of his predecessor Pope Martin I.[23] It is also for this reason that Pope St. John XXIII (1958-1963) convoked the Second Vatican Council (1962-1965) and did not see the First Vatican Council (1869-1870)'s definition of papal infallibility as something that makes councils obsolete.

In other words, Eastern Orthodox Christians need not consider various organs of infallibility obsolete or redundant. Rather, the Orthodox should see them as consistent with their own Scripture and the witness of the first millennium.

3

"Every bishop is a successor of St. Peter, not just the pope"

Orthodox generally maintain that every bishop in the world is a successor of the apostle Peter, not by a direct line of ordinations that trace back to Peter, but insofar as each of them represents Peter's authority among his flock. In other words, in the same way that Peter exercised a leadership role among the rest of the apostles, each local bishop exercises a leadership role among his flock.

The Catholic Church agrees with the Orthodox that each bishop represents Peter's authority among his own flock, but the Church also claims that the bishop of Rome exercises a unique authority over all Christians as a direct successor of Peter. So the pope exercises a leadership role among the bishops.

I remember once having a theological discussion with a non-Catholic Christian online. I mentioned that Christians, as members of the New Covenant, are given the Holy Spirit and adopted as children of God (Gal. 3:26). I was immediately met with resistance and told, "Everyone is a child of God!"

It is certainly true that there is a general sense in which everyone is created by God and thus a child of God. Yet

Scripture notes that some are children of wrath (Eph. 2:3), which is contrasted with the children of God mentioned in Galatians. In other words, there is a sense in which all are children of God, and another sense in which only covenant members are children of God.

Without distinctions, the difference between the children of wrath and the children of God becomes obliterated in the claim that all are children of God—though this may be true in a general sense. In other words, if we merely focus on the general sense in which all are children of God, we will miss the unique sense in which New Covenant members are children of God.

So it is with the Orthodox claim that all bishops are successors of Peter, not just the bishop of Rome.[24] There is a general sense in which this is true, but there is also a special sense in which the bishop of Rome is the unique successor of Peter. Unfortunately, this unique sense has been overlooked by many in Orthodoxy, who think the general sense excludes the unique sense.

This phenomenon in Orthodox apologetics is by no means new. For instance, the fourteenth-century metropolitan of Thessalonica, Nilus Cabasilas, expresses this common Orthodox argument: "Christ has founded his Church on the profession of Peter and on all those who have been the guardians of this profession."[25]

Catholic historian Fr. Francis Dvornick (1893-1975) unpacks the implications of this argument:

> These guardians are the bishops who thus all become successors of St. Peter. The result of this interpretation is clear: the universal Church is represented by the bishops who, because they are all the successors of Peter and profess his faith, are equal![26]

At first, the faith of some Catholics may be shaken when they discover this argument, especially since there is evidence in the first millennium that every bishop was considered a successor of Peter, in a general sense. For instance, St. Cyprian of Carthage (210-258) testifies to this view in the third century:

> Our Lord, whose precepts and admonitions we ought to observe, describing the honor of a bishop and the order of his Church, speaks in the Gospel, and says to Peter: "I say unto you, that you are Peter, and upon this rock will I build my Church; and the gates of hell shall not prevail against it. And I will give unto you the keys of the kingdom of heaven: and whatsoever you shall bind on earth shall be bound in heaven: and whatsoever you shall loose on earth shall be loosed in heaven."[27]

But with the proper distinctions, this position is ultimately reconcilable with what the Catholic Church claims about the pope.

Catholics agree that every bishop, in a general sense, is a successor of Peter in his own diocese, insofar as every bishop professes the same faith as what Peter professed in Matthew 16:16 and is a leader among his flock. Yet this does not detract from a unique sense in which the pope is the successor of Peter. What is this sense? In the same way that Peter was head of the apostolic college, as Orthodox historically have admitted in their acceptance of the Council of Ephesus, which says as much,[28] so too the bishop of Rome is the head of the college of bishops. It is inconceivable to say that every bishop is the head of the college of bishops, as you can't have every single member of a group also be the leader of that group.

This is effectively the position of Philip the papal legate at the third ecumenical council, the Council of Ephesus (431), which both Catholics and Eastern Orthodox consider authoritative. Before the assembly of council fathers, which was mostly composed of Eastern bishops, the papal legate exclaimed,

> We offer our thanks to the holy and venerable synod, that when the writings of our holy and blessed pope had been read to you, the holy members by our holy voices, ye joined yourselves to the holy head also by your holy acclamations. For your blessedness is not ignorant that the head of the whole Faith, the head of the apostles, is blessed Peter the apostle.[29]

In the same council, he says,

> There is no doubt and in fact it has been known in all ages, that the holy and most blessed Peter, prince and head of the apostles, pillar of the Faith, and foundation of the Catholic Church, received the keys of the kingdom from our Lord Jesus Christ the Savior and Redeemer of the human race, and that to him was given the power of loosing and binding sins: who down even to today and forever both lives and judges in his successors. The holy and most blessed pope Celestine, according to due order, is his successor and holds his place, and us he sent to supply his place in this holy synod, which the most humane and Christian emperors have commanded to assemble, bearing in mind and continually watching over the Catholic faith.[30]

How did the council fathers react to Philip's claims? Orthodox scholar Fr. Alexander Schmemann says that when the fathers of the council heard his words, "the Greek bishops remained silent."[31]

It should be noted that in these quotes, the legate clearly identifies Pope Celestine as the successor to Peter in a way that does not apply to the other bishops. Otherwise, if every bishop present at the council were a successor of Peter in the exact same way, then it would have been meaningless to liken Celestine to Peter, the head of the apostles, and it would have been meaningless to say the council fathers joined themselves to their head—that is, the pope. And if some interpret the council fathers' silence to mean disapproval, then that becomes problematic, as it would mean that the council fathers failed to correct error in their midst. For this reason, the silence must be interpreted as agreement.

Clearly, the papal legate drew a parallel between Peter's relationship to the apostolic college and the pope's relationship to the college of bishops manifested at the Council of Ephesus. For this reason, the claim that every bishop is, generally speaking, a successor of Peter in his own diocese is not diametrically opposed to the claim that the popes are unique successors of Peter when acting in their position over the universal Church.

4

"The Church Fathers did not teach the *filioque*"

The Church Fathers are revered Christian leaders and saints from the East and the West who lived in the early Church (first to eighth centuries). Both Catholics and Orthodox highly venerate them as insightful witnesses to the Faith.

The *filioque* refers to the Catholic teaching that the Holy Spirit receives his nature from the Father and the Son. Many Catholics recite the Nicene Creed with a later added clause that affirms the *filioque*.

Some Orthodox believe that the *filioque* is heretical and should not be recited in the Nicene Creed. Other Orthodox affirm that the *filioque* may be a true teaching but tend to stress that Catholics should not have added it to the Nicene Creed without the consent of the Orthodox.

All Catholics affirm the truthfulness of the doctrine of the *filioque*, but not all Catholics recite it in the Nicene Creed, and some are of the opinion that those who do are creating an unnecessary stumbling block for reunion with the Orthodox.

I was once asked what I believed was the worst conceivable punishment that should be given to the most egregious criminal offenders in the name of justice. I said, "Assigning the criminal the task of comprehending the difference between Catholics and Orthodox on the *filioque*."

Considering that simply understanding the debate on the *filioque* is a feat of its own, I do not expect to solve that debate here. However, there may be a shortcut to determining who is right. To discover the answer, it is important to work through the question of whether the Church Fathers taught the *filioque* and, if so, to draw some conclusions from this.

Before we proceed, it might be helpful to define terms. What is the *filioque*? Simply put, *filioque* is a Latin clause added to the Nicene Creed by the Western churches. This clause says the Holy Spirit "proceeds from the Father *and the Son*." According to the *Catechism of the Catholic Church* (CCC), which quotes the Council of Florence, the concept behind this clause is as follows:

> The Holy Spirit is eternally from Father and Son; he has his nature and subsistence at once (*simul*) from the Father and the Son. He proceeds eternally from both as from one principle and through one spiration. . . . And, since the Father has through generation given to the only-begotten Son everything that belongs to the Father, except being Father, the Son has also eternally from the Father, from whom he is eternally born, that the Holy Spirit proceeds from the Son (246).

In other words, the Father and the Son, as one act, eternally *spirate*—that is, breathe out—the Holy Spirit. However, the Son does not have the ability to participate in this act in and of himself, as he is eternally begotten of the Father and receives from the Father the ability to spirate the Holy Spirit. For this reason, we can say the Holy Spirit has his source (*arche*) in the Father, even if the Son plays a mediatory role.

Now that we have defined our terms, did any of the Church Fathers teach this doctrine?

Some Orthodox will claim that the answer is an emphatic *no.* This can be seen vividly in the Encyclical of the Eastern Patriarchs of 1848, where the patriarchs of Constantinople, Alexandria, Antioch, and Jerusalem all claim that the doctrine of the *filioque* cannot be defended from the Church Fathers.[32] At first, a Catholic inquiring into Eastern Orthodoxy may be concerned about this, especially considering that the same patriarchs claimed that the Catholic doctrine of the *filioque* is heretical![33] But is this true?

It is certainly the case that the Church Fathers in the West taught the *filioque.* This is why the Eastern Orthodox scholar Edward Siecienski can say that the Eastern fathers at the reunion Council of Florence in the fifteenth century were at a disadvantage: they had to engage "over a millennium of Latin writing supporting the *filioque.*"[34]

Among the Western Fathers listed by Siecienski as supporting the *filioque,* St. Augustine of Hippo (354-430) is pre-eminent.[35] The late Metropolitan Kallistos Ware (1934-2022) agrees that Augustine taught the *filioque* and identifies Augustine's teaching as the understanding of the *filioque* presented by the Catholic Church at the Council of Florence.[36]

These Orthodox scholars, among others, are incredibly confident that Augustine taught the *filioque* because the saint is so explicit in his view on the subject. For instance, Augustine says,

> If, therefore, that also which is given has him for a beginning by whom it is given, since it has received from no other source that which proceeds from him; it must be admitted that the Father and the Son are a Beginning (*principium*) of the Holy Spirit, not two Beginnings (*duo*

principia); but as the Father and Son are one God, and one Creator, and one Lord relatively to the creature, so are they one Beginning relatively to the Holy Spirit. But the Father, the Son, and the Holy Spirit is one Beginning in respect to the creature, as also one Creator and one God.[37]

It is not Augustine alone who expressed the *filioque* in the West. Siecienski maintains that Eucherius of Lyons (380-449) carried the torch of Augustine's *filioque*.[38] Others, such as Gennadius of Marseilles (d. 496), Julianus Pomerius (d. 505), and Avitus of Vienne (450-519), all gave evidence that they maintained the *filioque*. This is why Siecienski can say that "by the late sixth century, the *filioque* achieved a level of acceptance in the West bordering on unanimity."

There are even Eastern Fathers, such as St. Gregory of Nyssa (335-395), who taught something similar to the *filioque*. Gregory said that the Holy Spirit "proceeds from the Father through the Son."[39] St. Maximus the Confessor (580-662) says,

For the Holy Spirit, just as he belongs to the nature of God the Father according to his essence so he also belongs to the nature of the Son according to his essence, since he proceeds inexpressibly from the Father through his begotten Son.[40]

Elsewhere, Maximus says,

From this they showed that they themselves do not make the Son the cause of the Spirit for they know that the Father is the one cause of the Son and the Spirit, the one by begetting and the other by procession, but they show the progression through him and thus the unity of the essence.[41]

Orthodox are certainly aware of quotes like these, and some say the quotes refer to an "eternal manifestation of the Holy Spirit by the Son."[42] The meaning of this latter position is incredibly esoteric, as it often depends on a philosophical difference between essence and energies and would require a lengthy treatise of its own to adequately explain. However, it effectively means that the Holy Spirit has his hypostatic origin in the Father alone but is made manifest energetically through the Son just as light is made manifest by a ray from the sun but the light has its ultimate source in the sun, not the ray.

Suffice it to say that it is hardly apparent that this was the original intention of the early Eastern Fathers when they affirmed that the Spirit proceeds from the Father through the Son. This is why Orthodox theologian Fr. Andrew Louth can say,

> Neither the eighth-century doctrine of the necessity of making and venerating icons nor the fourteenth-century Palamite distinction between essence and energies can really be found in the fourth-century Fathers.[43]

Others argue that the Eastern Fathers did admit that the Holy Spirit proceeds from the Father through the Son, but only in relation to his work within creation (this is known as the *economic Trinity*),[44] and not from eternity past within God (which is known as the *immanent Trinity*).[45] For Catholics, the order of operations in the economic Trinity is reflective of the immanent Trinity. Additionally, there are elements in John 16:12–15 and Revelation 22:1 that indicate that the Holy Spirit's mediation through the Son is immanent.

Regardless of how the early Eastern Fathers viewed the role of the Son in relation to the Holy Spirit, the *Western* affirmation of the *filioque* presents a difficult problem for the Eastern Orthodox. In the first millennium of the Church's history, the Orthodox were in communion with the Western bishops who maintained the *filioque*. This means that modern Orthodox must either condemn the Western Fathers—men as venerable, in both East and West, as Augustine, Pope Leo I (440-461), and Fulgentius of Ruspe (462-533)—for teaching heresy or admit that the *filioque* is a tolerable doctrine. If they claim that the Western Fathers and saints taught heresy, then they must admit they were in communion with heretics for many centuries. Not to mention they have to explain why the ecumenical councils in the first millennium that took place after Western reception of the *filioque* did not condemn the doctrine of the *filioque* as heretical.

Some Catholics have noted the implications this has on the East in venerating Western saints who taught the *filioque*. One Catholic author notes,

> It would do no less than severely damage the veracity of either Catholicism or Orthodoxy, both of which hold to the Patristic East and West as their saintly heritage of faith.[46]

This is why some Orthodox today maintain that the Catholic view on the *filioque* can be reconciled with the Orthodox view of the Holy Spirit, and that it can be maintained as a *theologoumenon*—that is, a legitimate theological opinion.[47]

Since there is a wide range of views among the Orthodox on the *filioque*, due to not having formulated a view on the procession of the Holy Spirit apart from the context of responding to the West,[48] a considerable number of Orthodox believe that this is a legitimate option. At the very least, it allows for the Orthodox to escape the charge of being in communion with heretics or condemning the view of so many of the venerable Fathers and saints in the West.

Some may ask, if the *filioque* doctrine is native to the first millennium, and many in the East were content to be in communion with the Western *filioquists*, then why did it become a source of contention between East and West in later centuries? I believe that Orthodox author and priest Fr. John Panteleimon Manoussakis answers adequately:

> Such a mystery as the procession of the Holy Spirit was dragged into the mud of the polemics between the two sides in order not to cause but to justify an estrangement already underway. It came to serve as an accusation that either side could throw at the other, precisely when such an accusation was needed. It became an excellent example of theology at the service of political divisions.[49]

Unfortunately, rather than being content to be in communion with those who hold to the *filioque*, as were many of the Eastern Fathers in the first millennium, some in Eastern Orthodoxy today see the conflict over the *filioque* as an occasion to question whether Catholics and Eastern Orthodox even believe in the same God![50]

If it is true that the *filioque* is heretical or presupposes a different God from that of Christianity, then a Catholic discerning Eastern Orthodoxy should honestly question how the Eastern Fathers, which the Orthodox uphold reverently, were in communion with Western Fathers, many of whom are saints in Orthodoxy, if they truly taught heresy and professed a different God. If they are not willing to come to the conclusion that the West taught heresy or another God, then what kind of damage does this do to Eastern Orthodox teaching authority, since the Encyclical of the Eastern

Patriarchs of 1848 condemned the *filioque* as heretical? If the patriarchs of Constantinople, Alexandria, Antioch, and Jerusalem, along with the entire Synod of Constantinople, the Synod of Antioch, and the Synod of Jerusalem, were all wrong in their evaluation of heresy in 1848, why should the Orthodox be a reliable guide to orthodox doctrine today? It would seem that the Orthodox must either admit they were wrong to condemn the *filioque* or admit that their teaching authority is unreliable.

5

"Catholics believe in a literal purgatorial fire"

Purgatory is the post-mortem purification for those who die having been forgiven for their sins but have not yet shed all attachments to sin.

Orthodox are divided on the specifics of the state of the afterlife before the second coming of Christ. Some would affirm a post-mortem purification of some sort, whereas others would reject such a notion.

Catholics affirm the existence of a purgatorial state for those who die in God's embrace but had an attachment to sin up to the moment of their death. The specific nature of this state (a literal fire, an encounter with Christ, etc.) is open for debate among Catholics.

There he was: a German Dominican friar, slowly entering a little town full of impressionable people, riding a white horse and surrounded by drummers and banner-carriers. He slowly ascended a makeshift stage the town had built for him, where he began to preach about the dreadful fires of the afterlife. To prove his point about the horrors of the fire, he placed his hands over an open flame until they were severely burned. The audience gasped in horror and were ready to do anything to avoid the eternal fire.

At least, that is how the 2003 movie *Luther* depicted John Tetzel's preaching.

Many people in Catholic circles have this kind of fire in mind when the "fires of purgatory" come up in discussion. But, as Eastern Orthodox author Clark Carlton says,

> The very idea of a temporal, purgatorial fire is unknown in Orthodoxy. The only fire spoken of in the scriptures is the fire of Gehenna—the permanent abode of the unrighteous *after* the universal resurrection and Final Judgment.[51]

This is also how the Orthodox at the reunion Council of Florence in the fifteenth century understood the Catholic doctrine of purgatory. In his work *The Council of Florence*, Joseph Gill describes the Orthodox perception of the Catholic view of purgatory as follows:

> The Greeks welcomed the Latin statement that the just go to heaven and the reprobate to hell. The Greeks likewise recognize a remission of sin after this life; but the question is the means by which that is produced. Certainly not by fire, for no Greek doctor ever mentions such, and teaching of that kind is dangerous as savoring the Origenist heresy, which taught that the fires of hell are not eternal, and as tending to relax the vigilance of the faithful.[52]

In other words, the Orthodox at the Council of Florence were not concerned about a post-mortem remission of sins *per se*. Rather, they were perplexed by talk of fire as a means to bring about such remission. The Orthodox were worried that the Catholics believed something foreign to their tradition and that the fires of hell are temporary.

This latter claim is entirely unfounded, as the Catholics had already proposed in the constitution *De Fide Catholica* at the Fourth Lateran Council (1215) that the reprobate will suffer "perpetual punishment with the devil."[53] Yet the contention that fire as a means of remitting sins after death was foreign to the Greek tradition may raise a few eyebrows for Catholics considering Orthodoxy.

Some of the Western Fathers, such as Gregory the Great, who is a saint in Eastern Orthodoxy, taught that there is a "purifying fire" for those who die in a state of venial sin.[54] It is true that such language cannot be found in the Eastern Fathers, but whether there are Eastern Fathers who use such language is not entirely decisive, since the Eastern Fathers were in communion with the Western Fathers—which vouches for the latter's orthodoxy.

Does the Catholic Church actually teach the doctrine that some suffer a purgatorial fire before being admitted into heaven? If so, is this fire a literal fire? The renowned Catholic theologian Ludwig Ott (1906-1985) rightly notes that the Church has never officially *defined* purgatory to be a literal fire:

> Out of consideration for the separated Greeks, who reject the notion of a purifying fire, the official declarations of the councils speak only of purifying punishments (*poena purgatoriae*), not of purifying fire.[55]

In other words, what is defined in Catholicism is that those who have committed venial sins at the time of death will undergo purification. That's it!

It is an acceptable opinion in Catholicism that this purification is through fire, but even the nature of this fire varies among those who hold to this opinion. Some say that the fire is literal, whereas others say it represents an encounter with Christ. For instance, here is what Pope Benedict XVI (2005-2013) has to say in his encyclical *Spe Salvi* (Saved in Hope):

> Some recent theologians are of the opinion that the fire which both burns and saves is Christ himself, the Judge and Savior. The encounter with him is the decisive act of judgment. Before his gaze all falsehood melts away. This encounter with him, as it burns us, transforms and frees us, allowing us to become truly ourselves (47).

This view is based on Sacred Scripture, which speaks of God as a "consuming fire" (Heb. 12:29).

We've covered what the Orthodox *don't* teach about purgatory. So what *do* they teach? Metropolitan Kallistos Ware speaks of various views. One of them is certainly consonant with the view expressed by Benedict XVI above:

> The majority would be inclined to say that the faithful departed do not suffer at all. Another school holds that perhaps they suffer, but, if so, their suffering is of a purificatory but not an expiatory character, for when a person dies in the grace of God, then God freely forgives him all his sins and demands no expiatory penalties: Christ, the Lamb of God who takes away the sin of the word, is our *only* atonement and satisfaction. Yet a third group would prefer to leave the whole question entirely open."[56]

The first view above may be compatible with the Catholic view, depending on how "suffer" is defined. The

Catholic position does speak of "purifying punishments," as noted above, but can be seen as the experience one has of encountering a pure and holy God. Might this encounter be seen as producing suffering? Perhaps, insofar as the encounter with Christ detaches us from any lingering attachments to sin. However, if what one means by *suffering* is the same kind of pain the damned will experience in the Lake of Fire, then this is not something that any Catholic is required to believe. Understood this way, the Catholic and Orthodox views of purgatory may be in harmony.

The second Orthodox view would slightly differ with Catholics, who affirm an expiatory nature to purgatory for any temporal guilt the individual may still have. The criticism Ware expresses for the Orthodox who hold to the second view is that it detracts from Christ, who is our only atonement and satisfaction. Orthodox priest Fr. Laurent Cleenewerck confirms this criticism, saying, "In this framework, Christ is not involved in this final purification."[57] However, this seems to be a straw man against the Catholic view, because Catholics believe that their acts of reparation, both in this life and in the afterlife, have their source in Christ and God's grace. No good that a Catholic does is ever, strictly speaking, meritorious in God's eyes. It is only because of the work of the Son of God, an abundance of grace, and the indwelling of the Holy Spirit that a sinner is able to perform acts of reparation for his sins.

Even the third view expressed above, too, is potentially compatible with the Catholic view, as it leaves the entire question open for discussion.

There is one more view among the Orthodox, though Kallistos Ware says that only rarely do Orthodox Christians hold to it today. This fourth view is a complete affirmation of the Catholic view of purgatory, which was expressed by the Confession of Dositheus, promulgated by the Synod of Jerusalem of 1672 in its eighteenth decree.[58] This synod is described by Ware as one of the "Orthodox doctrinal statements," though he notes that only some of it has been accepted, whereas other parts have been "set aside or corrected."[59]

Philip Schaff (1819-1893) summarizes decree eighteen of this synod as follows:

> The souls of the departed are either at rest or in torment, according to their conduct in life; but their condition will not be perfect till the resurrection of the body. The souls of those who die in a state of penitence (μετανοήσαντες), without having brought forth fruits of repentance, or satisfactions (ἱκανοποίησις), depart into Hades (ἀπέρχεσθαι εἰς ᾅδου), and there they must suffer the punishment for their sins; but they may be delivered by the prayers of the priests and the alms of their kindred, especially by the unbloody sacrifice of the Mass (μαγάλα δυναμένης μάλιστα τῆς ἀναιμάκτου θυσίας), which individuals offer for their departed relatives, and which the catholic and apostolic Church daily offers for all alike. The liberation from this intervening state of purification will take place before the resurrection and the General Judgment, but the time is unknown.[60]

Once more, this may not be a popular position among the Orthodox today, but it shows that Orthodoxy does have affirmations of the Catholic doctrine of purgatory in its history.

Orthodox author and priest Fr. Andrew Damick also concedes that Orthodoxy has a concept of post-mortem purgation. He says,

Orthodoxy agrees that there is a certain purgation needed for the souls of the departed destined for heaven, but that experience has never been codified with the temporal model of years of suffering employed by Rome in the purgatory doctrine.[61]

Fortunately, Catholicism does not necessitate the view that purgatory should be considered in terms of "years," so this should not be a barrier between Catholicism and Orthodoxy. Plus, the affirmation of a post-mortem purgation in Orthodoxy is effectively an affirmation of purgatory. This can be seen in the Orthodox scholar Fr. Dumitru Stăniloae (1903-1993), who describes the Orthodox view of the afterlife as follows:

This makes it possible for those in hell who are not radically different from those on the lowest levels of paradise to pass over to paradise before the Last Judgment, through the prayers of the saints and those on earth. . . . Up until the Last Judgment, those in hell who do not totally lack faith in Christ can also be moved to the paradise of communion with Christ. . . . These are persons who through their kindness and their reduced faith did not commit acts that damaged the life and salvation of others—acts such as homicide; abortions; unbecoming sexuality outside marriage; depriving others of necessary things . . . or those who repented of these things before death but not in a degree corresponding to their evil deeds.[62]

In other words, there are some who die with faith in Christ but are imperfectly penitent. These souls can be aided by the prayers of the faithful, which will result in them being transitioned from hell to heaven before the Final Judgment. This is exactly the Catholic view of purgatory, as *hell* can refer to purgatory in Catholic theology, among its other usages. For instance, the *Catholic Encyclopedia* notes four different usages for the term *hell*, and one of them is purgatory.[63]

The Catholic view also says there is no post-mortem repentance for those who die impenitent, but Stăniloae is careful to note that this transition is only for those who have repented of grave sins before death, though imperfectly. The group Stăniloae describes refers not to those who die without repentance (the damned), nor to those who die perfectly penitent (the blessed), but to a third group that dies in a state of imperfection. Simply put, this is what Catholicism identifies as the souls in purgatory.

In summary, many Orthodox often take great pains to deny the Catholic doctrine of purgatory, even to the extent of denying their own councils—but the concept of purgation still finds its way into Orthodox theology. This means that the Orthodox may think they have a significantly different view of the afterlife from the Catholic view, but in reality, they hold to a doctrine that is essentially the same as the Catholic position. And so, the road to Catholic unity may be shorter than the average Orthodox realizes.

6

"Catholics believe that all men are guilty of Adam's sin"

Orthodox are divided on the question of the relationship between Adam's sin and the rest of humanity. All agree that Adam's sin in the Garden of Eden introduced human death in the world—so that all who are born of Adam are subject to human death. All also agree that humans born of Adam are not personally guilty of Adam's sin. However, many Orthodox maintain that everyone who is born of Adam inherits from him a weakened will that is inclined to sin. Lastly, some Orthodox prefer the term *ancestral guilt* rather than *original sin* in discussions about the consequences of Adam's sin.

The Catholic Church teaches that human death was introduced into the world because of Adam's sin. It also teaches that all who are born of Adam have lost the original holiness and moral uprightness that humanity had in Adam before his sin in the Garden of Eden. The Church also teaches that every individual is responsible for his own sins, and nobody inherits the personal guilt Adam incurred through his sin.

A common criticism of Catholicism by some in Eastern Orthodoxy is that Catholics believe that all humans are

guilty of Adam's sin. Metropolitan Kallistos Ware expresses this in his work *The Orthodox Church*: "Most Orthodox
theologians reject the idea of 'original guilt,' put forward by
Augustine and still accepted (albeit in a mitigated form) by
the Roman Catholic Church."[64]

In this section, Ware is measured in his criticism of Catholicism compared to some in Orthodoxy, as he says Catholics hold to a form of ancestral guilt that is more "mitigated" than Augustine's version, which is that infants, who
die deprived of baptism, suffer mildly in hell. Ware does
not specify what this "mitigated form" is, but any form of
ancestral guilt imputed to the human race because of the sin
of Adam sounds unjust and absurd to most Catholics today.

Does the Catholic Church teach that God attributes
guilt to mankind because of the sin of Adam in the Garden
of Eden? This claim most likely comes from a misunderstanding of the Council of Trent. In its fifth session, it says
the following:

> If anyone says that the guilt of original sin is not remitted
> through the grace of our Lord Jesus Christ which is given
> in baptism, or even asserts that all which pertains to the
> true essence of sin is not removed, but declares it is only
> erased and not attributed: let him be anathema.[65]

It is true that the council refers to the "guilt of original
sin," but this is not the best translation. The Latin word
used by the Tridentine fathers is *reatum*. This word should
be distinguished from *culpa*, from which we get the word
culpable. *Reatum* refers to a state or condition, not necessarily
a personal fault. For instance, Lewis and Short's Latin
Dictionary defines it as "the condition of an accused
person, a state of impeachment."[66] There is certainly a

difference between the state mankind finds itself in after the fall of Adam and personal guilt for Adam's personal sin.

In other words, the Catholic Church teaches that the human race inherits a particular condition from Adam, but not personal culpability for his sin. The *Catechism of the Catholic Church* says,

> Although it is proper to each individual, original sin does not have the character of a personal fault in any of Adam's descendants. It is a deprivation of original holiness and justice, but human nature has not been totally corrupted (405).

In other words, original sin is a deprivation of something, not personal guilt for someone else's sins. Understood this way, Catholics and Orthodox may not have a conflict, as Orthodox author Fr. Andrew Damick says:

> A true inherited guilt is more characteristic of certain streams in Protestantism than it is of Rome. Yet the identification of original sin as inherited guilt in Catholic theology nevertheless persists in Orthodox polemics.[67]

Ironically, the Confession of Dositheus, which was accepted at the Eastern Orthodox 1672 synod in Jerusalem, teaches that the descendants of Adam are subject to eternal punishment through the inheritance of original sin. In decree sixteen, the confession states,

> And since infants are men, and as such need salvation, needing salvation they need also baptism. And those that are not regenerated, since they have not received the remission of hereditary sin, are, of necessity, subject to

eternal punishment, and consequently cannot without baptism be saved.[68]

It is up to the Eastern Orthodox to determine the meaning and the level of authority this statement carries for their churches, but this should give pause to a Catholic who is discerning Eastern Orthodoxy if he is concerned about the Catholic position on original sin.

It should also be noted that the Orthodox canonical tradition has accepted a canon from the Council of Carthage, held between 418 and 419, which explicitly teaches the Catholic doctrine of original sin. The canon states,

> It has pleased the council to decree that whosoever denies the little ones newly born from the wombs of their mothers when they are being baptized, or asserts that they are baptized for the remission of sins, but that they have inherited no original sin from Adam obliging them to be purified in the bath of renaissance (whence it follows that in these persons the form of baptism for the remission of sins is not true, but is to be regarded as factitious), let him be anathema; for no other meaning ought to be attached to what the apostle has said, viz., "Sin entered the world through one human being" (Rom. 5:12), and thus it passed over into all human beings; wherefore all of them have sinned, than that which the Catholic Church diffused and spread abroad everywhere has ever understood those words to mean. For it is on account of this canon of the Faith that even the little ones too, who are as yet incapable of committing any sin of their own to render them guilty of any offense, are truly baptized for the remission of sins, in order that what sin they inherited from the primordial birth may be purified in them through the process of renaissance.[69]

Note that the canon admits that sin is inherited through birth and is remitted by baptism, which is why Catholics and Orthodox baptize infants for the remission of sins. However, as stated before, this must be understood as a deprivation of holiness and justice, not as personal guilt for the sin of Adam. Understood in this sense, Orthodox should avoid seeing original sin as a barrier between Catholicism and Orthodoxy.

Lastly, the Council of Ephesus (431), which the Eastern Orthodox accept as the third ecumenical council, condemned the position of Caelestius (fourth century), who was a disciple of Pelagius (354-418). Caelestius rejected the doctrine of original sin and the Church's practice of the baptism of infants. He was condemned in the council's seventh session as follows:

> If the metropolitan of a province, having distanced himself from this holy and ecumenical council . . . has embraced the doctrines of Caelestius or does so in the future, he can no longer act in any manner against the bishops of the province, since he is henceforth barred by the council from all ecclesiastical communion and is rendered completely ineffective.[70]

In other words, an ecumenical council accepted by the Orthodox affirms the doctrine of original sin by way of rejecting Caelestius's denial of this doctrine. For this reason, this doctrine should not be seen as a barrier between Catholics and Orthodox.

7

"The Immaculate Conception would mean that Mary did not die"

The Immaculate Conception is the Catholic teaching that the Blessed Virgin Mary was protected from the taint of original sin from the moment of her conception.

Orthodox hold the Virgin Mary in high regard. They tend to agree that she did not commit any personal acts of sin, but they are divided over whether she was free from original sin. Some are happy to affirm the doctrine of the Immaculate Conception. Others believe that the absence of original sin from the Virgin Mary at the moment of her conception means that she was not subject to human death. Since the Orthodox celebrate the Feast of the Dormition, which commemorates the death and assumption of the Virgin Mary, the doctrine of the Immaculate Conception is seen as a denial of the feast—and is thus rejected.

Catholics affirm the doctrine of the Immaculate Conception but do not believe that the absence of original sin from the moment of the Virgin Mary's conception automatically means that she was exempt from some of the effects of the fall—such as human death.

As early as the sixth century, parts of Eastern Christendom began celebrating a liturgical feast on the theme of the death and assumption of the Virgin Mary. This feast was known as the Feast of the Dormition of the Theotokos and is celebrated to this day in the East and the West by Catholics and Orthodox. However, in the Western tradition, the element of Mary's *dormition*—that is, her death—is not emphasized, as the feast tends to focus on her bodily assumption into heaven.

What does this have to do with the Immaculate Conception? One objection some Eastern Orthodox tend to raise concerning the Immaculate Conception is that it necessarily means that the Virgin Mary did not die, which is certainly in conflict with the liturgical tradition of the East. So, some Orthodox conclude that the Immaculate Conception is a false teaching of the Catholic Church. Orthodox author and priest Fr. Andrew Damick puts it this way:

> Probably the clearest argument against the Immaculate Conception, however, is that the Virgin Mary died—involuntarily and by necessity. If she had been born without the effects of original sin, then she would have been incapable of death.[71]

Potential Catholic converts to Orthodoxy may find this kind of argumentation convincing, especially considering that the Immaculate Conception was defined as a dogma as late as the nineteenth century. In the eyes of some, this late definition of the dogma may be perceived as a novelty that contradicts the ancient Feast of the Dormition.

However, the case against Catholicism is not as strong as it may seem. Does the dogma of the Immaculate Conception truly necessitate the view that the Virgin Mary did not die?

The above argument assumes that Catholics teach that a human may suffer death only if he has contracted original sin. Certainly, this flies in the face of Christ's death, burial, and resurrection! Yet some may retort that Christ's death was voluntary, and Mary's was involuntary, indicating that the latter died of necessity due to her contraction of original sin. In fact, Fr. Damick above assumes this kind of argumentation when he asserts that the Virgin Mary died "by necessity." Damick merely asserts this position and does not give any reasons to believe it, but let's assume he's right for the sake of the argument. Does this mean that the Virgin Mary contracted original sin? No! Catholic theologian Ludwig Ott rightly notes,

> Freedom from original sin does not necessarily involve freedom from all defects which came into the world as a punishment for sin.[72]

One such defect is death. The *Catholic Encyclopedia* explicitly states this:

> The state of original sanctity, innocence, and justice, as opposed to original sin, was conferred upon [Mary], by which gift every stain and fault, all depraved emotions, passions, and debilities, essentially pertaining to original sin, were excluded. But she was not made exempt from the temporal penalties of Adam—from sorrow, bodily infirmities, and death.[73]

In other words, the Immaculate Conception means that the Virgin Mary did not contract the internal defects that resulted from the Fall, such as disordered desires, but she was subject to some of the Fall's external effects.

Another curiosity to common Orthodox apologetics in this area is the claim that Catholics believe either that the Virgin Mary did not die or that this question is open for debate. For instance, Orthodox author Clark Carlton says that "the papal bull defining the dogma of the Assumption (*Munificentissimus Deus*) is deliberately vague about whether or not she actually died."[74] The implication here is that the teaching is deliberately vague because the matter of whether Mary died is open for debate in Catholicism. However, Pope Pius XII, in publishing *Munificentissimus Deus* (Most Bountiful God), was not deliberately vague in this matter. In the context of the teaching of the Fathers, he commends them, saying,

> However, since the liturgy of the Church does not engender the Catholic faith, but rather springs from it, in such a way that the practices of the sacred worship proceed from the Faith as the fruit comes from the tree, it follows that the holy Fathers and the great Doctors, in the homilies and sermons they gave the people on this feast day, did not draw their teaching from the feast itself as from a primary source, but rather they spoke of this doctrine as something already known and accepted by Christ's faithful. They presented it more clearly. They offered more profound explanations of its meaning and nature, bringing out into sharper light the fact that this feast shows, not only that the dead body of the Blessed Virgin Mary remained incorrupt, but that she gained a triumph out of death, her heavenly glorification after the example of her only-begotten Son, Jesus Christ—truths that the liturgical books had frequently touched upon concisely and briefly (20).

Perhaps the pope is vague in the definition about the end of the Virgin Mary's earthly life, but he is not vague about it in the rest of the document when he speaks of her "dead body."

Carlton, familiar with Catholics who claim that Mary died and not knowing how to respond to this inconsistency in his argumentation, retorts,

> This, however, makes no sense whatsoever. If the Virgin is exempt from the guilt of Adam's sin and possesses the original justice, then it would be *unjust* for her to be subject to the temporal penalty of sin. Hence the vagueness of the definition.[75]

Once again, Carlton doesn't account for the rest of the papal document, which does speak of the death of the Virgin Mary. Moreover, the claim that it would be unjust for the Virgin Mary to experience death if she had not contracted original sin is similar to the argumentation atheists use against Christians when they say a just God would never allow his son to be crucified, or a just God would never create people who he foreknew would spend eternity in the Lake of Fire. In the same way that it was not unjust of God the Father to allow God the Son to die on the cross, though an injustice was committed by those who put him to death, we may say it was not unjust for God to allow Mary to be subject to some of the effects of the fall of Adam, though Adam's ushering in of death into the world was a personal act of injustice on his part.

As an aside, it is inconsistent for some Eastern Orthodox to argue against the Immaculate Conception when it may be found in their tradition. Fr. Andrew Damick says, "The Orthodox do hold to a pre-purification of the Virgin Mary, not at her conception but at the Annunciation."[76] This doesn't account for important Orthodox figures who affirm the Immaculate Conception, among whom, per the Eastern Catholic scholar Fr. Christiaan Kappes, is George-Genna-dius Scholarius (d. 1473), a patriarch of Constantinople who was a vocal critic of the reunion Council of Florence. In fact, Kappes says that Scholarius "often speaks about the Im-maculate Conception of the BVM [Blessed Virgin Mary]."[77] If an Orthodox Christian, or even a Catholic discerning Orthodoxy, is troubled by the Immaculate Conception in Catholicism, he will then have to grapple with the presence of this doctrine in Orthodoxy.

Moreover, there are modern Orthodox, such as Fr. John Panteleimon Manoussakis, who see the dogma of the Immac-ulate Conception as compatible with their tradition. He states,

> The doctrine that proclaims that the Mother of God was sanctified at her conception comes to declare simply what every Christian, Orthodox or Catholic, has always be-lieved about the person of the Theotokos, namely, that in her we find the most perfect human being—better yet, in her we see the true nature of a human person, a nature unafflicted by any sin, including the original sin.[78]

In summary, Orthodox apologetics against the Immacu-late Conception often assumes a faulty definition of original sin, does not account for papal recognition that the Virgin Mary died, and does not account for its own tradition on the matter.

8

"The Immaculate Conception implies that Mary had a different nature from the rest of humanity"

On one occasion, I was scrolling through social media and came across an Orthodox elder and author who made this claim. He argued that the Catholic doctrine of the Immaculate Conception means that the Virgin Mary had a different nature from the rest of humanity, which in turn means that the human nature Jesus took from the Virgin Mary is different from the rest of humanity's. This view would lead to the position that Jesus did not redeem the human race, since he did not take up our human nature in the Incarnation.

I immediately thought the Orthodox monk failed to appreciate that Catholics explicitly affirm that the Virgin Mary has the same nature as the rest of humanity. In the apostolic constitution *Ineffabilis Deus* (Ineffable God), which defines the Immaculate Conception, the Church clearly states,

> For it was certainly not fitting that this vessel of election should be wounded by the common injuries, since she,

differing so much from the others, had only nature in common with them, not sin.

Perhaps an Orthodox will say that Catholics are inconsistent on this point. But I would add that I was also baffled by how the Orthodox gentleman could reason through the implications of this position in his diatribe against Catholicism but fail to see the implications of his own assumption in the critique.

For example, if we argue that the Immaculate Conception—the claim that the Virgin Mary was free from the stain of original sin from the moment of her conception—necessarily means that the Virgin Mary had a different nature from the rest of humanity, then that assumes that original sin is part of human nature. This is an absurd position, since it would mean that Adam and Eve had a different nature from the rest of humanity, which is problematic, given that Jesus is the "New Adam." It would also mean that Jesus had a different nature from everyone else, since he was free from the stain of original sin. This would lead to the unwanted consequence that Christ healed a nature other than our own, which would make the Incarnation pointless and salvation impossible— which is ironically what the Orthodox claim Catholics are guilty of in affirming the Immaculate Conception.

The Orthodox elder had not thought through this argument as carefully as we might hope. So it is with many Orthodox who repeat this common argument against the Catholic teaching of the Immaculate Conception. Since Catholics are clear in rejecting the claim that the Virgin Mary had a different nature from the rest of humanity, Orthodox should avoid leveling this accusation against Catholics and instead seek to understand how Catholics harmonize these things.

9

"Created grace makes God a created being"

One of the most common arguments a Catholic inquirer into Orthodoxy will encounter is the claim that Catholicism believes in created grace. For the Orthodox, the claim is that a person receives God's uncreated grace through the reception of the sacraments. Consequently, this puts a person in touch with the uncreated—that is, God. However, Orthodox claim that Catholics maintain something different with the concept of created grace. This concept is understood by some Orthodox to mean that God does not really communicate himself to creatures in the giving of grace through the sacraments, so recipients of God's grace always remain alien to him. After all, they argue, if what a person receives in the sacraments is a created substance, then a person doesn't really encounter the uncreated God. It is then concluded that this leads to atheism—that is, the claim that there is no God—and it will then be conveniently pointed out that Western society has drifted into atheism over the last few centuries.

There are many problems in this chain of argument. Let's consider two: whether the notion of created grace means that God does not communicate himself in giving grace and whether Catholicism actually teaches that grace is created.

We may speak of grace as *uncreated* and *created*. Uncreated grace is God himself. Created grace is the effect produced in the recipient of God's uncreated grace—also God himself. In the latter case, grace is a subjective state rather than a thing. In other words, that which recipients of grace receive is truly God, but this reception of grace produces in them a new state of being, which we call *created* (since the creature did not exist that way prior to the reception of grace).

Some Eastern Orthodox do not understand this, and so they ask, "Is the grace by which man is saved a created phenomenon or the uncreated energy of God?"[79] As seen above, the answer would be that the grace we receive is truly God, but the state that reception produces in us creatures is a created effect. This is why Catholic theologian Ludwig Ott says,

> The hypostatic union, the indwelling, and the beatific vision, considered as acts, are indeed created graces, for they had a beginning in time. But the gift which is conferred on a creature in these acts is uncreated.[80]

This is usually recognized by more informed Orthodox, such as Fr. Andrew Damick, who says the following about the proper understanding of created grace in Catholicism:

> The Orthodox should have no strong objection to that, though we might advise picking a different word than *grace* for the "analogical" effect. "Created grace" language is actually used in some of the Orthodox Fathers.[81]

Consequently, Orthodox who use this argument against Catholicism tend to do so based on the mistaken idea that Catholics are saying that the thing received by the creature is some created thing rather than God himself.

Moreover, Catholics are not obliged to use the language of *created grace*, since it has never been put forth by the Catholic Magisterium (teaching authority) as something Catholics must adhere to. This is why Fr. Damick also says of created grace,

> It's important to note that while there are difficulties with this language, it is not a dogmatic teaching held by Rome and so could be worked out more easily in relations with the Orthodox.[82]

Far from being a matter of contention, this issue truly boils down to a difference in terminology.

10

"Development of doctrine means Tradition can change"

> *Doctrinal development* is the idea that doctrine revealed by God, or doctrine intimately related to revealed doctrine, may develop over time, but it cannot evolve, change, or be corrupted. Doctrinal development is analogous to a seed organically growing into a full-grown tree. Doctrinal *corruption* is analogous to a dog transforming into a cat.
>
> Orthodox are divided on the question of doctrinal development. Some argue that it is impossible, whereas others are happy to admit it and even offer examples of doctrinal development in Eastern Orthodoxy. However, all Orthodox agree that doctrine does not evolve.
>
> Catholics believe in doctrinal development but reject doctrinal evolution or corruption.

Catholics often take for granted the claim that doctrine can develop over time. However, a Catholic inquirer into Orthodoxy will most likely be surprised to find out this is not the case within some quarters of Orthodoxy. For instance, Orthodox priest Fr. Daniel Lattier surveys Orthodox writers on the question and discovers some who claim that "there exists an Orthodox consensus against doctrinal development."[83] Fr.

Lattier does not necessarily agree with this, but he points out that it is a claim made by some prominent Orthodox.

Part of the problem in this discussion is defining what Catholics mean by *development of doctrine*. Certainly, some Orthodox have misunderstood what Catholics mean by this, as Fr. Lattier says:

> Some of the Orthodox rejections of DD [development of doctrine] are attributable to misunderstandings about what DD means, which is probably further attributable to a lack of engagement with primary sources on DD.

There is often an ignorance among the Orthodox about the development of doctrine because they are not familiar with the key documents from Catholics on the concept. Another problem is a failure on the part of some Orthodox to see its roots in the Patristic era. Additionally, for those Orthodox who deny such development, it is hard to claim there have been no doctrinal developments in Eastern Orthodoxy in the last 2,000 years. Let's examine each of these problems briefly.

What do Catholics mean by development of doctrine? Some Orthodox think it means that Catholics add to the deposit of faith—that is, God's divine revelation handed down to us through his Son and the apostles. In reality, this is not what Catholics mean by development of doctrine. Consider this definition from a Catholic encyclopedia:

> Nothing has been added to or subtracted from the deposit of faith since the death of the last apostle. However, the mysteries revealed by Christ to his apostles are clearer now than they were in the first centuries, through the penetration of these truths by the early Fathers and Doctors of the Church.[84]

This means that Catholics do not add to divine revelation handed down by Christ and the apostles, but further penetrate its mysteries and implications, especially when new questions arise. For instance, Jesus and the apostles never taught that the use of artificial contraception in a marriage is immoral. Yet that does not mean that the use of contraception would be permitted according to the standard of divine revelation, since it can be argued that the use of contraception would violate certain biblical moral principles. Likewise, it is highly unlikely that the apostle Paul bowed down and kissed icons of the Blessed Virgin Mary. However, it would be wrong to say that the theology that allows for one to venerate icons is foreign to Paul. It is in this sense that one can agree with the seventh ecumenical council (787), which appeals to the apostles for its dogmatic definition on the veneration of icons.

One thing to stress here is that the deposit of faith never changes. There can never be a development that would substantially break with the Faith handed down by the apostles. If such a thing were to happen, then it would no longer be development we are referring to, but corruption or evolution. Thus, the deposit of faith must always remain substantially the same in every age, but certain implications of the Faith may emerge at a later time.

Are there Patristic roots for this concept? In fact, there are! St. Vincent of Lérins (d. 445) said the following in the fifth century:

But someone will say, perhaps, "shall there, then, be no progress in Christ's Church?" Certainly; all possible progress. For what being is there, so envious of men, so full of hatred to God, who would seek to forbid it? Yet on condition that it be real progress, not alteration of the Faith.

For progress requires that the subject be enlarged in itself, alteration that it be transformed into something else.[85]

Note two elements here. One is *progress* or *development*. This refers to some kind of change. Yet this concept is mitigated by the claim that there are to be no *alterations* to the Faith.

Think of a small human child growing into an adult. It is true that there are some developments and progress to the child's growth. However, one cannot say such changes constitute alterations to the person's substance, since this would mean the human child no longer remains human, but becomes something else, like a tree. Clearly, it is impossible to have a human child change into a tree and to simultaneously claim there have been no substantial changes to the child.

Understood in this sense, the notion of development of doctrine is thoroughly Patristic and consistent with Eastern Orthodoxy's understanding of the deposit of faith. This is why Fr. Lattier can say St. John Henry Newman's thesis of doctrinal development, which builds upon Vincent of Lérins, is consistent with Eastern Orthodoxy.[86]

Lastly, are there instances of progress, or development, in Eastern Orthodoxy? It is hard to deny that there are, considering the importance of icon veneration.

It is undeniable that first-century Christians were not bowing down to icons. If they were, this would have undoubtedly been the most frequently used criticism the Jews, who took the Old Testament's proscription of "graven image[s]" (Exod. 20:4) seriously, would have leveled against them. Yet there is no evidence of such criticism, let alone evidence of icon veneration among the early Christians. However, as noted above, the framework for such things is certainly apostolic. It is in this sense that the Second Council of Nicaea can say,

Likewise also I venerate and honor and salute the relics of the saints as of those who fought for Christ and who have received grace from him for the healing of diseases and the curing of sicknesses and the casting out of devils, as the Christian Church has received from the holy apostles and Fathers even down to us today.[87]

Moreover, the doctrine of the essence and energies of God, as expressed by the Eastern Orthodox saint Gregory Palamas (1296-1359), has been argued by some to be a development of the theology of some of the Eastern Church Fathers. A good case can be made that it is substantially consistent with some theological streams in the Patristic era. However, it is hard to deny that there was some progress made by Palamas. For this reason, and as we saw in our fourth objection, Orthodox theologian Fr. Andrew Louth says,

Neither the eighth-century doctrine of the necessity of making and venerating icons nor the fourteenth-century Palamite distinction between essence and energies can really be found in the fourth-century Fathers.[88]

In other words, when properly understood, development of doctrine is not only something Orthodox should not oppose, but something they have to acknowledge in their own churches.

11

"Jesus forgives sins, not a priest"

Orthodox believe that it is Christ who forgives the sinner of his sins when he repents and confesses. Orthodox offer the sacrament of confession for people who wish to confess their sins, and they teach that forgiveness is obtained through this sacrament, though they tend to stress that it is Christ who forgives the sin and the priest who is present during the sacrament is a witness.

Catholics affirm everything above but tend to emphasize the mediatory role of the priest in the sacrament of confession. The priest is not one who forgives sins by his own authority, but he mediates God's grace and forgives sins by the authority of Jesus.

In Orthodoxy, confession is usually done in front of an icon of Jesus and the book of the Gospels. The penitent confesses his sins to Christ while the priest stands beside the penitent and listens as witness to his confession. After the confession of the penitent, some advice may be given by the priest, and then he places his *epitrachelion* (stole) over the penitent's head and says a prayer of absolution. In some churches, the prayer is active—that is, "I forgive"—and in others, it may be passive—"may God forgive."

With this understanding in mind, we come to an odd objection raised by some Orthodox against Catholics on the sacrament of penance. Catholics are used to Protestants' criticism against the Catholic concept of confession, with objections like "God alone forgives sins, not a priest!" But it may be alarming for a Catholic to discover that some Orthodox use similar objections.

For instance, Metropolitan Kallistos Ware describes the Orthodox perspective of confession as follows:

> This outward arrangement [the penitent confessing in front of an icon of Jesus and the Gospels] emphasizes that in confession it is not the priest but God who is the judge, while the priest is only a witness and God's minister.[89]

Notice how God and the priest are juxtaposed, treated as if they are in opposition. The underlying assumption is that God does not act as a judge through the priest, but acts apart from the priest, and the latter is merely a witness.

Compare this to the *Catechism of the Catholic Church*, which says, "The priest is the sign and the instrument of God's merciful love for the sinner" (1465). In the Catholic perspective, the priest *does* act as a witness to God's judgment—and he *also* is the instrument of God's judgment. This seems to be an example of an either/or versus both/and mentality that sometimes finds its way into certain quarters of Eastern Orthodoxy.

Curiously, Ware notes that there have been moments in Orthodox history where the both/and approach was taken by Orthodox priests who used a prayer of absolution found in some Slavonic books, which says, "I forgive," rather than "May God forgive," which was more common in the Greek formula.[90] Ware notes that some Orthodox look down on this language, though it is admittedly found in parts of Orthodox history. Thus, it need not be something absolutely foreign to the Orthodox churches.

Moreover, though the commonly used prayer of absolution in the Orthodox churches has elements that are passive, the service books that have active language are not seen as contradictory to the passive language. Consider this from the Rite of Confession by the Antiochian Orthodox Christian Archdiocese of North America:

> May our Lord and God Jesus Christ, through the grace and bounties of his love toward mankind, forgive thee, my child, N., all thy transgressions. And I, his unworthy priest, through the power given unto me by him, do forgive and absolve thee from all thy sins, in the name of the Father, and of the Son, and of the Holy Spirit. Amen.[91]

Note the passive language, "May our Lord . . . forgive thee," and the active language, "I . . . absolve thee." This shows that the Orthodox who do use the active formula see it as complementary with the passive language. In other words, they are able to see the Orthodox priest not as "only a witness," as Ware notes above, but also as an instrument of God's forgiveness.

Similar to the Orthodox, some of the Eastern Catholic churches, which are in communion with the pope, also have passive and active language in the rite of confession. For instance, in the *Small Euchologion* in use in the Byzantine Catholic Church, the prayer of absolution reads,

May our Lord and God, Jesus Christ, by the grace and mercies of his love toward mankind, forgive you all your transgressions. And I, a priest, though unworthy, by his power given to me, forgive and absolve you from all your sins, in the name of the Father, and of the Son, and of the Holy Spirit.[92]

Once again, note the complementary "May our Lord . . . forgive you," and "I . . . absolve you" language. Catholics too are comfortable using both passive and active language in the rite of confession, because the priest acts both passively, as a witness of God's grace, and actively, as an instrument of God's mercy.

PART 2

HISTORICAL ATTACKS

Many discussions between Catholics and Orthodox revolve around historical matters. This is because both Catholics and Orthodox believe that the Holy Spirit guides the Church through all ages of Church history and creates holy men and women who testify to Jesus' message. These holy figures, most notably the Church Fathers and Doctors, are visible landmarks for Christians to look back to for guidance. They serve as signposts to orthodox Christianity.

Likewise, Church councils play a significant role—not only because they are historical landmarks of orthodoxy, but because they teach the Christian faith authoritatively. Consequently, discussions between Catholics and Orthodox often involve questions related to Church councils and the Fathers.

In what follows, we will examine historical objections raised by the Orthodox, often revolving around those holy figures and landmark events.

12

"The Eastern churches in the first millennium never accepted papal infallibility"

Orthodox (and Protestants) often argue against papal infallibility by saying that it was not accepted by the Eastern churches of the first millennium. Some Catholics who discern Orthodoxy and encounter this objection may have their faith in the divine institution of the papacy challenged as a result. Yet is it true?

Before directly answering this objection, it is important to define our terms. By *papal infallibility* one does not mean that the pope is impeccable in all his acts. Neither does it mean he is incapable of erring in matters of science. Rather, it simply means that, under certain conditions, his teachings on matters of faith and morals are free from error.

The bishops of the First Vatican Council (1859-1870) explain this concept as follows:

We teach and define as a divinely revealed dogma that when the Roman pontiff speaks *ex cathedra*, that is, when, in the exercise of his office as shepherd and teacher of all Christians, in virtue of his supreme apostolic authority, he defines a doctrine concerning faith or morals to be held by the whole Church, he possesses, by the divine assistance promised to him in blessed Peter, that infallibility which the divine Redeemer willed his Church to enjoy in defining doctrine concerning faith or morals.[93]

Clearly, with so many qualifications, the doctrine of papal infallibility is significantly limited in scope. From the text of the council, it applies only when the pope speaks on a matter of faith and morals, as pastor of the universal Church, and with the intention of definitively binding the universal Church.

Having established a proper definition of papal infallibility, we may now examine the objection. It is certainly true that the modern Eastern Orthodox churches reject papal infallibility. However, there are several instances where the Eastern churches accepted papal infallibility, which is intimately tied to the concept of Roman indefectibility, expressed in the first millennium. The case of the Formula of Hormisdas (519) may be considered as one example, but first, a little background is in order about the controversy settled at the fourth ecumenical council known as the Council of Chalcedon (451).

What exactly was the controversy that the council had been called to resolve? It was whether Christ had one or two natures. Though the council fathers at Chalcedon affirmed Christ's two natures, the language the council used gave some the impression that it taught the heresy of *Nestorianism* (i.e., that Jesus is two persons), which had been previously condemned at the Council of Ephesus (431). This was simply a misunderstanding, since the heresy of Nestorianism was preoccupied with the claim that Jesus was two *persons*, and Chalcedon was about Jesus having two *natures*. Due to linguistic barriers, Chalcedon's affirmation of two natures sounded like Nestorius's affirmation of two persons.

In order to fix the fallout between Chalcedonian and non-Chalcedonian Christians, the emperor Zeno (425-491) released the *Henoticon* (482), a document that attempted to straddle the fence between the two camps. In this document, the emperor condemned Nestorius but did not explicitly affirm Chalcedon's teaching about Christ's two natures. Both sides were dissatisfied.

Meanwhile, the patriarch of Constantinople, Acacius (d. 489), persecuted Christians who did not adopt the *Henoticon*, which led to his condemnation by the pope. After several decades of schism, the new emperor, Justin I (450-529), pushed for reunion between Rome and Constantinople. Rome was willing—yet this would come at a cost! Pope St. Hormisdas (514-523) sent a confession of faith to the emperor, requiring his signature, along with that of the patriarch of Constantinople and many other Eastern bishops. This confession of faith, known as the Formula of Hormisdas, states the following:

> The beginning of salvation is to preserve the rule of a correct faith and to deviate in no respect from the constitutions of the Fathers. And because the teaching of our Lord Jesus Christ cannot be allowed to fail, who said, "Thou art Peter, and upon this rock I will build my Church," etc. [Matt. 16:18], these things which were said are proved by the effects of things, because in the Apostolic See religion has always been preserved without spot or blemish.[94]

Hormisdas clearly asserts that the true Faith may be known by the doctrinal decisions of the See of Rome.

Some might push back and say the formula merely attests to Rome's orthodoxy unto the present and is silent about whether it will remain orthodox in the future. This seems to be an untenable interpretation, since the formula situates the claim to Rome's orthodoxy in the context of the promise that Christ made to the apostle Peter in Matthew 16:18. In other words, Rome has remained orthodox unto the present because of Christ's promise to Peter—a promise that cannot be broken, since it rests on the authority of Jesus. Thus, the formula's claim is that just as Christ's promise to Peter cannot be broken, so too it is that Rome cannot lose its doctrinal purity.

Amazingly, the Eastern bishops signed the formula!

Some push back and note that there were various versions of the formula circulated and signed in the East. This is true, yet the variants differ not on the papal claims made in the formula, but on the names of the bishops who were condemned in the Acacian Schism.[95] Moreover, if the formulas signed by the Eastern bishops removed the papal claims, as some Orthodox wrongly assert, then that means that the Easterners knew they were in communion with a pope who maintained the papal claims, which the East today considers heretical. This would mean that those who removed the papal claims in the East shared in the pope's heresy by knowingly communing with a heretic. If the East could compromise in such a way, upon what basis can one say the East held the Faith?

The Catholic historian Robert Eno thinks the Formula of Hormisdas is noteworthy for its claims about the papacy. He states,

> The formula of reunion put forward by Pope Hormisdas is noteworthy for a phrase that is significant not just in the history of Roman primacy, but more specifically for the pre-history of papal infallibility.[96]

Nor are only Catholics convinced of this. The Anglican priest and scholar Henry Chadwick (1920-2008) explicitly admits the connection between the papal claims of primacy and infallibility in the Formula of Hormisdas and the First Vatican Council: "His formula was to enjoy later echoes and to be restated by the First Vatican Council in 1870."[97]

But what is shocking is that Eastern Orthodox theologians, too, recognize that this was a victory for Catholic ecclesiology, as it was the background for the First Vatican Council's claim to papal infallibility. This is why Fr. Alexander Schmemann, an Eastern Orthodox theologian, writes,

> Even more characteristic of this eternal compromise with Rome was the signing of the formula of Pope Hormisdas by the Eastern bishops in 519, ending the thirty-year schism between Rome and Constantinople. The whole essence of the papal claims cannot be more clearly expressed than in this document, which was imposed upon the Eastern bishops.[98]

Likewise, Orthodox author Edward Siecienski admits that this is "one of the strongest affirmations of Rome's teaching authority accepted in the East."[99]

On occasion, some have pushed back on the example of the Formula of Hormisdas by saying Patriarch John II of Constantinople (d. 520) signed the document only with the understanding that his see was equal to Rome, saying,

> I accept the fact that the two most holy churches, that is to say, that of Ancient Rome and that of the New Rome, should be one; I admit that the see of St. Peter and that of the imperial city should be one.[100]

Even some Catholic scholars have seen this preface by John as a way of asserting the equality of the sees of Rome and Constantinople.[101] However, this is an incredibly unlikely interpretation in light of the fact that the divine promises of indefectibility made to Peter and his successors, as expressed by the formula, could hardly be considered applicable to the see of Constantinople, considering the various occasions in which its patriarch embraced heresy.

What, then, did John mean? Simply put, his remark that the sees of Constantinople and Rome "should be one" meant that they should be in agreement. This is the interpretation that Msgr. Pierre Batiffol (1861-1929), a French Catholic priest and theologian, makes in his remarks on the matter: "But, as a matter of fact, this preface did not touch the formula, and affirms the union which John declares that he desires between his see and that of Rome."[102]

Moving beyond this example of papal infallibility, another may be found in the acts of an ecumenical council accepted by both Catholic and Eastern Orthodox Christians. This council is the Third Council of Constantinople (the sixth of the seven councils both Catholics and Orthodox accept), which was held from 680 to 681, and it combated the heresy that Christ has only one will. At the council, Pope Agatho merely reasserted the definitive decision of his predecessor, Martin I. This reassertion was made in a letter from the pope to the emperor, which was read out loud before the council fathers.

Agatho's letter not only reasserts Rome's definitive decision on this Christological controversy, but also asserts Rome's indefectibility in matters related to the Faith. Not surprisingly, the pope locates the guarantee of this indefectibility in the words of Christ. The letter states,

> For this is the rule of the true Faith, which this spiritual mother of your most tranquil empire, the apostolic Church of Christ, has both in prosperity and in adversity always held and defended with energy; which, it will be proved,

by the grace of Almighty God, has never erred from the path of the apostolic Tradition, nor has she been depraved by yielding to heretical innovations, but from the beginning she has received the Christian faith from her founders, the princes of the apostles of Christ, and remains undefiled unto the end, according to the divine promise of the Lord and Savior himself, which he uttered in the holy Gospels to the prince of his disciples: saying, Peter, Peter, behold, Satan has desired to have you, that he might sift you as wheat; but I have prayed for you, that [your] faith fail not. And when you are converted, strengthen your brethren.[103]

It continues:

Let your tranquil Clemency therefore consider, since it is the Lord and Savior of all, whose faith it is, that promised that Peter's faith should not fail and exhorted him to strengthen his brethren, how it is known to all that the apostolic pontiffs, the predecessors of my littleness, have always confidently done this very thing: of whom also our littleness, since I have received this ministry by divine designation, wishes to be the follower, although unequal to them and the least of all.

Note that the pope asserts that his predecessors, who are called the "apostolic pontiffs"—that is, the popes—have preserved the Faith in the matter of Christ's two wills, since the Faith is guaranteed by the words of Christ to Peter, who promised that his faith would not fail. This is a clear reference to Roman indefectibility, which would later be defined at the First Vatican Council as papal infallibility.

It is also noteworthy to mention the reaction of the council fathers to Pope Agatho's letter. Rather than reject his claims about Roman indefectibility as heresy, they explicitly praise his words:

> Therefore to you, as to the bishop of the first see of the universal Church, we leave what must be done, since you willingly take for your standing ground the firm rock of the Faith, as we know from having read your true confession in the letter sent by your fatherly beatitude to the most pious emperor: and we acknowledge that this letter was divinely written (*perscriptas*) as by the chief of the apostles, and through it we have cast out the heretical sect of many errors which had recently sprung up, having been urged to making a decree by Constantine who divinely reigns, and wields a most clement scepter.[104]

At this point, some may claim that the fathers of this council were simply being strategic by not condemning Agatho's claims about the Roman See. After all, they certainly needed Rome's aid in stamping out the heresy of Monothelitism (the heresy that Christ has one only will), so it would have been unwise to challenge Rome on this matter. Rather than this being a way to redeem the credibility of the Eastern bishops present at this council, if true, this would make them disingenuous. Consequently, their witness to orthodox Christology would surely be destroyed.

Moreover, contemporaneous sources in the East testify to papal infallibility. For instance, the highly venerated Eastern saint Maximus the Confessor affirmed the divine establishment of papal infallibility as follows:

> For the very ends of the earth and those in every part of the world . . . look directly to the most holy church of the Romans and its confession and faith as though it were a sun of

unfailing light, expecting from it the illuminating splendor of the Fathers and sacred dogmas. . . . All the churches of Christians everywhere have held the greatest Church there to be their sole base and foundation, since, on the one hand, it is in no way overcome by the gates of Hades according to the very promise of the Savior, but holds the keys of the orthodox confession and faith in him . . . and, on the other hand, it shuts up and locks every heretical mouth that speaks unrighteousness against the Most High.[105]

Some Orthodox will push back and say Maximus did not believe in papal infallibility, since he was asked what he would do if the Roman church communed with the heretical church of the Byzantines. Maximus responded, "The Holy Spirit, according to the apostle, condemns even angels who sanction anything against what has been preached."[106]

Maximus references Galatians 1:8, where Paul says that an angel from heaven, or even he himself, would be condemned if he preached another gospel. Does this verse from Paul mean he denied his own infallibility when writing under the inspiration of the Holy Spirit in Sacred Scripture? No, as it is possible to rhetorically say that even a sacred author, who has the charism of infallibility when under the inspiration of the Holy Spirit, may be condemned if he were to deny the gospel. This does not mean that Paul actually believed that it would happen. Likewise, for Maximus to use this kind of rhetorical argument does not actually mean he believed that Rome had defected from the Faith or did not possess infallibility in certain instances. In fact, as shown above, he believed that it would be protected from such error since, he claimed that the gates of hell would not prevail against the Roman church because of the promise of Christ.

This places Eastern Orthodox Christians in a difficult predicament. The Orthodox must either admit that the Eastern bishops at the Third Council of Constantinople, and saints like Maximus the Confessor, were orthodox in their acceptance of papal infallibility, or claim that these Eastern Fathers accepted heresy.

13

"The case of Pope Honorius disproves papal infallibility"

I vividly recall having a conversation with an Orthodox priest about papal infallibility. When I broached the subject, he immediately said, "The popes aren't infallible. The case of Pope Honorius proves that!" I gently offered some pushback, hoping to show him that his overly confident response was premature. To his credit, he listened attentively and mulled the information over, and he realized that the case was not as clear has he had thought.

Sadly, his simplistic objection and knee-jerk reaction are not uncommon when the topic of papal infallibility comes up. Catholics, Orthodox, and Protestants often overestimate the case of Honorius in discussions about papal infallibility, believing that it is a clear-cut case that invalidates the claims of the First Vatican Council. However, the objection loses all force when we consider how papal infallibility is defined.

So who is Honorius, and how does he bear on the Orthodox interpretation of papal infallibility?

We can find the answers to these questions in the seventh century, when the Church was rocked with the debate over whether Christ had one will (*Monothelitism*) or two wills (*Dyothelitism*). Far from a trivial theological debate, the controversy had deep theological implications. For example, if

Christ has only one will, then that means his will is either divine or human. If it is divine, then Christ did not take on a human will—which means mankind's will has not been restored and remains fallen. If Christ took on a human will but did not retain his divine will after the Incarnation, then it can't be argued that God became incarnate, but only some part of God—since God has a will. This position is absurd, since God is not made of parts and can't be divided into parts.[107] It would also mean that God, who is immutable, has changed in some way by losing his divine will.

Due to the importance of these Christological issues, Patriarch Sergius of Constantinople (d. 638) wrote to Honorius I (625-638), asking for his theological advice on the matter. In a reply to the patriarch in the year 634, Pope Honorius writes, "We confess one will of our Lord Jesus Christ."[108] This certainly gives the appearance that he accepted the later condemned heresy of Monothelitism.

As noted above, if the pope had, in fact, accepted the error of Monothelitism, it would mean that either Christ lost his divine will or didn't redeem the will of humans in the Incarnation.

However, the context of what Honorius meant by "one will" is not what was condemned later by the Third Council of Constantinople. Catholic theologian Joachim Salaverri, S.J., succinctly explains the difference: "Honorius is speaking about the will of Christ, not as *physically* one but as *morally* one, because of the perfect agreement of the two natural wills of the Son of God."[109]

This is the view of Pope John IV (640-642), in his apology for Honorius, written in the spring of 641, just two years after Honorius died. The apology—not a request for forgiveness, as the modern understanding of the word *apology* suggests, but rather a defense—notes,

My aforementioned predecessor [Honorius], in his teaching on the mystery of Christ's incarnation, was saying that there were not in him opposing wills of the mind and flesh, as there are in us sinners. But certain people, changing it to their own meaning, suspected him to have taught one will of his divinity and humanity, which is the complete opposite of the truth.[110]

Additionally, St. Maximus the Confessor (highly venerated by both East and West) came to Honorius's defense in his famous disputation with the Monothelite Pyrrhus (d. 654). His argument was that the same secretary who transcribed Honorius's letter later explained that Honorius was arguing not for Monothelitism, but against the view that Christ had two conflicting wills in his humanity.[111]

So, what do we make of the sixth ecumenical council, which condemned Honorius as a Monothelite? Fr. Francis Dvornik, a respectable Catholic scholar and Church historian, notes of this council,

This very same council, at the same time as it condemned the Monothelites, condemned Pope Honorius, since the letters which Honorius had sent to Sergius had been wrongly interpreted as favorable to Monothelitism.[112]

Does this mean that the council erred in its judgment of the person of Honorius? Some Orthodox will say such a claim is unheard of in the first millennium and is something Catholics in the second millennium have conveniently created to explain away the case of Honorius in light of the Church's claim about papal infallibility. However, consider the position the ninth-century papal archivist Anastasius Bibliothecarius, where he writes the following about accusing the sixth ecumenical council of error: "Holy Pope Gregory indicated that this [council] was to be accepted only 'up to the issuing of the canons.'"[113] In other words, Bibliothecarius drew from Gregory the Great (540-604) that the sixth ecumenical council should be accepted in its canons, but other aspects of the council may be considered objectionable. So, the idea that an ecumenical council can err was not unheard of. But is such a thing possible, especially on a matter as consequential as the posthumous condemnation of a pope?

Given that Church doctrine guarantees infallibility only in matters of faith and morals, or matters of fact that are necessarily connected to a matter of divine revelation, it is certainly possible that the council erred in a matter of historical fact.

However, let us take it for granted that Honorius *did* support Monothelitism, and the council *did* rightly condemn him. Even then, the argument against papal infallibility fails, because the pope's response to Sergius does not meet the requirements for an *ex cathedra* teaching as described by the First Vatican Council. There are three:

1. The pope addresses a matter of faith and morals.

2. The pope defines the doctrine.

3. The pope binds the whole Church to the teaching.

In the case of Monothelitism, the pope did address a matter of faith and morals, and some argue that he intended to address the whole Church by his response—but there is no reason to believe he solemnly defined any doctrine, let alone Monothelitism. Thus, this instance fails to meet the criteria of papal infallibility.

Moreover, there is arguably some evidence for the position that Pope Leo II (682-683), who oversaw the council after

Agatho's death, ratified the council's judgment on Honorius only in the sense that Honorius was negligent and not someone who obstinately maintained a heresy. Salaverri states this argument as follows:

> Historically it is certain the body of bishops intended to condemn Honorius as a heretic together with other Monothelite heretics. . . . [But] the infallible definition cannot be said to be this body of bishops, because it is lacking the essential and necessary confirmation of the *head*, that is, the pope. . . . *The object* of the definition of the council confirmed by the pope was not the condemnation of Honorius of heresy, but of negligence in putting down the heresy.[114]

It should also be noted that the council fathers who condemned Honorius as a heretic did so after accepting Agatho's letter, which we discussed in objection 12 above. Recall that this letter declared not only that the teaching office of the Roman church is indefectible, but also that all of Agatho's predecessors (including Honorius) had preserved the Faith.

This would mean that either the council fathers contradicted themselves, or they saw Honorius as a heretic in his private person, and not in a way that defiled his teaching office as the pope. In fact, if they had believed that Honorius had defiled Rome's teaching authority, then upon what basis could they tolerate the claim of Leo II, who confirmed with Petrine authority the decisions of the council? The pope states:

> And because, as we have said, it has perfectly preached the definition of the true Faith which the Apostolic See of blessed Peter the apostle (whose office we unworthily

hold) also reverently receives, therefore we, and by our ministry this reverend Apostolic See, wholly and with full agreement do consent to the definitions made by it, and by the authority of blessed Peter do confirm them, even as we have received firmness from the Lord himself upon the firm rock which is Christ.[115]

It makes little sense to appeal to a Petrine authority to confirm a condemnation of Pope Honorius if the case of Honorius had demonstrated that the Apostolic See did not preserve Peter's faith in his day. This is more obvious when the council had already accepted that Peter's faith would be preserved in the apostolic pontiffs "undefiled unto the end," based upon Christ's promise to Peter in Luke 22:31–34. Once more, either the fathers contradicted themselves, or they did not see the case of Honorius conflicting with the credibility of the Apostolic See of Rome.

14

"Canon Six of Nicaea I is incompatible with the pope's claim to universal jurisdiction"

Orthodox believe that every bishop is tasked with leading his own diocese (a bishop's territory) and that no other bishop is able to interfere in his internal affairs without his consent. Orthodox recognize that there may be *metropolitans (archbishops)* and *patriarchs* who have an additional role of oversight over other bishops in their region, or nation, through the use of a synod of bishops (a group of bishops in a particular territory). However, they cannot directly interfere in the affairs of other bishops—though a synod of bishops may be able to depose or elect a bishop.

Catholics believe that every bishop is the ordinary leader of his own diocese and that other bishops cannot interfere in his internal affairs without his consent, except for the case of the bishop of Rome, who exercises a primacy and universal jurisdiction over the whole Church and is able to intervene in any diocese without the consent of the bishop. This is due to the pope's commission to govern the whole flock of God as the successor of St. Peter. However, the pope does not normally intervene in the affairs of a bishop unless there is a case of necessity.

Another favorite objection of some Orthodox, and even some Protestants, that a discerning Catholic will encounter concerns the sixth canon of the Council of Nicaea (325). Critics of Catholicism often claim this canon denies the papal claim to *universal jurisdiction*, which is the claim that the pope can intervene in the affairs of any bishop in the world without the bishop's consent.

Fr. Vladimir Guettée (1816-1892), a former Catholic priest turned Orthodox, wrote a polemic against the papacy in the nineteenth century. In this work, he articulates the argument as follows:

> First, the council [of Nicaea] declared that the authority of the bishop of Rome extended only over *a limited district*, like that of the bishop of Alexandria. Second, this authority was only based upon *usage*. Hence, it follows that this authority in the eyes of the council was not *universal*; that it was not *of divine right*. The ultramontane system, being entirely based upon the *universal* and *divine* character of the papal authority, is diametrically opposed to the sixth canon of the Nicene council.[116]

Before responding, it would be helpful to examine directly the text of the sixth canon of Nicaea. The canon reads,

> Let the ancient customs in Egypt, Libya, and Pentapolis prevail, that the bishop of Alexandria have jurisdiction in all these, since the like is customary for the bishop of Rome also. Likewise in Antioch and the other provinces, let the churches retain their privileges. And this is to be universally understood, that if anyone be made bishop without the consent of the metropolitan, the great synod has declared that such a man ought not to be a bishop. If,

however, two or three bishops shall from natural love of contradiction, oppose the common suffrage of the rest, it being reasonable and in accordance with the ecclesiastical law, then let the choice of the majority prevail.[117]

On the surface, the canon seems to assume a limited jurisdiction exercised by the bishop of Rome, since it refers to a limited territory for the bishop of Alexandria. However, when the context of the canon is understood, the apparent tension between the canon and the claims of the pope to universal jurisdiction disappear.

What was the context for this canon? The bishop of Alexandria had exercised a certain jurisdiction—namely, episcopal consecration—over the territories of Egypt, Libya, and Pentapolis, but this jurisdiction had been contested by Meletius (d. 327), the bishop of Lycopolis. The council sided with the established custom and justified its decision based on the precedent from the bishop of Rome. Fr. Francis Dvornik explains this precedent from Rome:

For Rome the situation was clear. In the diocese of Italy, the bishop of Rome exercised, in fact, a direct jurisdiction over all the bishops, without being obliged to pass through the metropolitans. It was natural that it be so in view of the intimate relation which existed between Rome and the cities of the diocese. These cities were only considered as *municipia*, whereas Rome, the capital, was *the City*.[118]

How does this clarify the matter and demonstrate that canon six does not oppose the claim to universal jurisdiction? Because the canon is referring not to the pope's universal jurisdiction, but rather to a different kind—that is, to the jurisdiction of the pope as a "suprametropolitan."[119] This is confirmed by Orthodox scholar Edward Siecienski, who also maintains that the canon is about the suprametropolitan level of authority.[120]

It should be remembered that the pope is first a bishop of a local diocese. He is then a patriarch (a suprametropolitan), and lastly the shepherd over the universal Church. The canon above describes his limited territory as a patriarch, but this is no more incompatible with his claim to universal jurisdiction than it is with his claim to be the bishop of the Diocese of Rome.

To put it simply, there is clearly a circumscription to the pope's authority when functioning merely as a bishop. After all, the pope does not claim to be the bishop of Nicaea or the bishop of Jerusalem! So too it is when he functions as a patriarch. However, when he is considered as functioning in his capacity as the shepherd of the universal Church, there is universal jurisdiction. In other words, when we regard the different roles the bishop of Rome has, talk of limited jurisdiction is not incompatible with claims to universal jurisdiction, because the concept of jurisdiction may be envisaged in different ways according to different roles.

Orthodox priest and scholar Fr. John Meyendorff, well aware of this argument, hesitates to accept these distinctions, claiming,

> Catholic historians . . . are often disturbed by this equality proclaimed between Rome and Alexandria by the Council of Nicaea, for, indeed, Rome is referred to as an example, not as a source of authority. This equality, according to them, applies only to the patriarchal privileges of the Roman See and not to its universal primacy. It is questionable, however, whether the Fathers of 325 would also have made that distinction.[121]

Would the fathers of Nicaea have made this distinction? The easy answer to this question is that they didn't have to!

If the fathers of the council were considering only the pope's patriarchal role, then their views about papal primacy were entirely immaterial to the canon. In other words, the canon neither confirms nor denies papal primacy as it was considering the bishop of Rome's role as a patriarch *only*.

Think of it like this. Suppose you have a man named Jim who is a brother, a husband, a father, and a grandfather all at the same time. Clearly (or at least hopefully), Jim is each one of these things in relation to different people. However, if his wife were to speak of him in a way that highlights his role as a brother, does that mean Jim's wife denies that he is also a husband, or a father, or a grandfather? Of course not! The reason is because Jim's role as a brother does not exclude the ability to consider Jim according to his other roles.

In fine, although it might be tempting to explore the views of the Nicene fathers on papal primacy, it is entirely unnecessary for the purposes of this particular objection. The claim that canon six negates papal primacy has not been sufficiently demonstrated. Thus, Catholics can simply shift the burden of proof back to the one who makes the claim.

15

"James led the Council of Jerusalem, not Peter"

Some Catholics are confounded when an Orthodox Christian denies papal primacy because of the role of St. James in relation to St. Peter at the first ecumenical council, the Council of Jerusalem (Acts 15:1–20). Some Orthodox claim that James, not Peter, had primacy among the apostles at the councils, and so the successors of Peter—that is, the popes—do not have any unique primacy over the successors of the apostles—the bishops.

Abbé Guettée, a Catholic convert to Orthodoxy, presents the argument as follows:

When the apostles assembled at Jerusalem, Peter spoke in council only as a simple member of the assembly, not even the first, but after many others. He felt himself obliged in presence of the other apostles—some old disciples and some faithful followers—to renounce publicly his opinion upon the necessity of circumcision and other Judaical ceremonies. James, bishop of Jerusalem, summed up the discussion, proposed the resolution which was adopted, and acted as the veritable president of the assembly. The apostles then did not consider St. Peter as the foundation stone of the Church.[122]

Echoing this argument, another Catholic convert to Orthodoxy, Michael Whelton, writes,

> Understandably, the Roman Catholic Church has always taught that Peter presided at the council but James held the episcopal See of Jerusalem. As we see in Acts 15, as befitting his role he (James) summed up the discussion and rendered the judgment. Hence, the obvious conclusion is that St. Peter's fellow apostles and leaders of the Jerusalem Christian community did not view him as the sole foundation stone of the Church.[123]

But is it so obvious? What Guettée and Whelton fail to note is that this is a straw man of the Catholic claim to papal primacy. After all, the pope is not absolutely required to preside over an ecumenical council. Granted, he does preside according to *modern* canon law (*Code of Canon Law*, 338 § 1), but this arrangement is certainly not a dogma of the Church. We know this because the Catholic Church accepts the second ecumenical council (381), which was presided over by Gregory Nazianzus (329-390) and later Meletius of Antioch (d. 381). Yet Catholics don't believe that this detracts from papal primacy.

Even when the pope does preside over an ecumenical council, it doesn't mean he must be the main figure there. For example, in the Second Vatican Council, there was a considerable amount of participation by the bishops, along with *periti* (theological experts), who had a hand in drafting some of the council's documents. Indeed, popes may not have any involvement in a council at all beyond its final ratification.

In other words, even if one were to grant that James presided over the Council of Jerusalem, which is a position that can certainly be challenged, it would not go against papal primacy, because the claim to primacy does not mean the pope has to take the lead or personally offer the final word in every council. However, there is still considerable evidence (e.g., the language used by Peter and James and the fact that Peter settles the debate) suggesting that Peter led the council in Jerusalem, not James.[124]

16

"Eastern Christians never really accepted that the pope had authority in the East"

Some Orthodox will claim that the Eastern churches never accepted that the pope had real authority in the East. Rather, the statements of Eastern bishops that seem to acknowledge his authority were merely occasions of Byzantine flattery—that is, adulation that was not meant to be taken literally. Eastern Orthodox author Edward Siecienski refers to this phenomenon as "rhetorical flourishes" that "have often been misunderstood."[125] According to Catholic priest and scholar Dom John Chapman, this phenomenon persisted even in his day, in the nineteenth century: "When the Council of Chalcedon wrote in a like strain to St. Leo, we are to put down its words as empty Oriental flattery." But, Chapman insists,

> Whatever may be thought of such comments, they cannot be applied to the words in which we have heard St. Maximus again and again set forth the privileges of Rome. Men do not shed their blood [as Maximus did—he was gruesomely tortured for defending Rome's teaching on Dyothelitism] to blunt a sarcasm or to justify a compliment.[126]

It is true that some of the Byzantines used flattery in their descriptions of the pope—and even the emperor! For instance, the bishops at a rival council to the Council of Ephesus (431), let by John of Antioch, wrote a letter to the emperors in their day with the following flattery:

> This, pious emperors, this is the confirmation of ortho-doxy. . . . We accounted the world most blessed in the imperial sway and authority with which it is governed. . . . Your injunctions exceed all admiration, most pious emperors. . . . We pray that your piety and your rule, nurtured in orthodoxy, may uphold and defend this or-thodox faith . . . for since the entire impulse of your rule is toward piety . . . may your Christ-loving head decree.[127]

Yet flattery does not account for all of the data in the first millennium, including the examples, referenced by Chap-man, of Pope Leo the Great and Maximus the Confessor.

Consider the case of Leo. The fathers of the Council of Chalcedon (451) lauded his tome against the heresy of Eu-tyches, saying,

> This is the Faith of the Fathers. This is the Faith of the apostles. We all believe accordingly. We orthodox believe accordingly. Anathema to him who does not believe ac-cordingly! Peter has uttered this through Leo.[128]

The council fathers seemingly indicate that Peter's au-thority manifested itself in his successor, Leo. If so, this would suggest they recognized that the pope had a Petrine authority that could be exercised in doctrinal matters, in-cluding in the East.

But what if all this was just overblown Byzantine flattery? In other words, some Orthodox contend that the fathers were merely lauding Leo's orthodoxy, but not literally claiming that Peter had spoken authoritatively through Leo.

But the evidence—the overwhelming evidence—blows the "flattery" justification apart. Indeed, key players at the Council of Chalcedon truly believed the pope could exercise authority in the East. For instance, when the council tried to push through canon twenty-eight, whereby the bishop of Constantinople attempted to usurp authority over the bishop of Alexandria, Leo immediately shut it down by his apostolic authority! He said,

> Indeed resolutions of bishops which are repugnant to the rules of the holy canons composed at Nicaea, in conjunction with the loyalty of your faith, *we dismiss as invalid, and by the authority of Peter, the blessed apostle, we absolutely disannul by a general decree* in all ecclesiastical cases.[129]

It should be stressed that this is an example of a pope annulling, by the authority of Peter, the canon of an ecumenical council formulated in the East. So the strong suggestion here is that the pope's authority not only extends to the East, but also takes precedence over an ecumenical council.

But it can be only a suggestion until we see how the Eastern authorities treated the pope's decree. After all, if they rebuked the pope, or rebelled, or forced their canon through, that could be a sign they rejected the pope's authority over an ecumenical council. So, what was the Eastern fathers' reaction to Leo's annulment of their canon? The bishop of Constantinople, Anatolius (d. 458), wrote back to the pope, saying,

As for those things which the universal council of Chalcedon recently ordained in favor of the church of Constantinople, let Your Holiness be sure that there was no fault in me, who from my youth have always loved peace and quiet, keeping myself in humility. It was the most reverend clergy of the church of Constantinople who were eager about it, and they were equally supported by the most reverend priests of those parts, who agreed about it. Even so *the whole force and confirmation of the acts was reserved for the authority of your blessedness.* Therefore let Your Holiness know for certain that I did nothing to further the matter, having always held myself bound to avoid the lusts of pride and covetousness.[130]

Here is an example of an Eastern bishop, no less than the occupant of the See of Constantinople, acknowledging the pope's authority in overruling a canon of an ecumenical council. To add to this, the emperor also submitted to Leo's decision.

Was this concession unique to Constantinople? No. Even the fathers of Chalcedon themselves, as they submitted their canon for the pope's ratification, wrote the following:

We therefore beg you to honor our decision by your assent, and as we have yielded agreement to the head in noble things, so may the head also fulfill what is fitting for the children.[131]

Note that they submitted their canon to the pope as a child submits his request to his head, his father. Clearly, important Eastern figures in this period believed that the pope had actual authority in Eastern affairs, not merely grandiose titles understood as mere Byzantine flattery.

What do Orthodox say in response to this? Orthodox scholar Fr. Alexander Schmemann dismisses it as a cowardly act on the part of the patriarch. He states,

> The protest of Pope Leo the Great against the twenty-eighth canon at Chalcedon (which made the See of Constantinople a "new Rome") was answered by Patriarch Anatolius with a cowardly renunciation of responsibility for the canon, assuring the pope that without the latter's approval not one of the decrees of the ecumenical council could be in effect.[132]

In other words, there is an admission that the patriarch yielded to the authority of the pope, though it was a "cowardly" act.

Events like these are why Orthodox author Edward Siecienski can say that some in the first millennium did embrace the papal claims. He notes,

> It may be that the co-existence of so many divergent views in the era of the "undivided Church" offers the most promise for future dialogue, as it allows both Catholic and Orthodox to acknowledge the Patristic roots of the other's approach. Both claim that their understandings of the primacy are grounded in the writings of the Fathers. Objectively speaking, both are correct, even if neither is completely right.[133]

In other words, one cannot simply wave everything away as mere instances of Byzantine flattery or rhetorical flourishes, since some in the early Church accepted the papal claims, whereas others rejected them. Similarly, some in the early Church accepted the divinity of Christ, whereas others rejected it. Frankly, dismissing papal authority in the first millennium under the guise of Byzantine flattery is similar to dismissing the divinity of Christ as early Christian flattery.

Now, if some early figures accepted papal authority over an ecumenical council and others rejected it, how can the issue be settled? In other words, when we are faced with what appears to be a lack of consensus in the early Church on a subject, what do we do? The Catholic will argue that Christ gifted the Magisterium (teaching authority) of the Catholic Church with the ability to settle such matters by discerning between things that deviate from the apostolic faith and things that are in accord with it.

For the Orthodox, no such Magisterium exists on the universal level—especially considering that they cannot consistently identify or hold an ecumenical council. So, no definitive judgment to bind the consciences of all Orthodox faithful can be forthcoming. Thus, for the Catholic there is a real solution—but for the Orthodox, there doesn't appear to be an identifiable mechanism to resolve such questions.

17

"The papal claims are historically dependent on forgeries"

It is often taken for granted by Orthodox that the papal claims made by the Catholic Church are historically dependent on forgeries. One of the most commonly cited examples is the Donation of Constantine, an eighth-century document that claims that the emperor Constantine gave Pope Sylvester (314-335) jurisdiction over all other bishops.[134] It is then argued that the papacy grew in authority only because of such forgeries, which is proof that the papal claims were not believed by Christians prior to the fabrication of the forgeries.

However, as we have seen, numerous saints and even ecumenical councils can be presented as witnesses to the papal claims before the eighth century. For instance, the fourth-century Church historian Eusebius (d. 339) wrote about Pope Victor, who lived in the second century. Eusebius notes that Victor threatened to excommunicate the churches of Asia for their practice of celebrating Easter at a different time from when the church of Rome celebrated it.[135]

Some Orthodox will point out that every bishop in the early Church had the authority to excommunicate other bishops from communion in his own local diocese. In fact, Orthodox author Edward Siecienski cites James McCue, who suggests that this was a mere excommunication from the local church of Rome, not the universal Church.[136] However, Eusebius notes that Victor threatened to cut the Asian churches off not just from communion with the church of Rome, but from "the common unity."[137] In other words, he was going to cut them off from unity with all of the churches.

Victor was criticized for this decision, but no one claimed that he was exceeding his authority. Moreover, this was clearly not an authority native to every bishop, as understood in Eastern Orthodoxy, as no Orthodox bishop has the authority to cut off another bishop from the common unity with all of the other Orthodox churches. Thus, well before the Donation of Constantine, the case of Pope Victor demonstrates that papal authority extended to the affairs of Eastern bishops.

Another example can be seen in 382, where the Council of Rome claimed infallibility for the church of Rome. It says,

> The holy Roman church has been set before the rest by no conciliar decrees, but has obtained the primacy by the voice of our Lord and Savior in the Gospel: "Thou are Peter and upon this rock . . . shall be loosed in heaven." . . . The first see of the apostle Peter is therefore the Roman church, "not having spot or wrinkle or any such thing."[138]

The council argues that Rome's primacy is based on the words of Christ, not conciliar decrees, and claims that Rome is free from any spot or wrinkle. It goes on to note that Alexandria and Antioch are also Petrine sees (in a different sense), but it makes no similar claim about them being free from spot or wrinkle.

In short, papal claims ultimately rest on the words of Christ. Any other arguments—appeals to canonical decrees, Rome's martyrs, Rome's status in the empire, papal forgeries—to explain the rise of the prominence of the papacy can only be seen as drawing out what the Church had already maintained.

Another proof of papal primacy from well before the Donation of Constantine is an epistle from Pope St. Boniface I (418–422) to the Eastern bishop of Thessalonica, Rufus. This epistle is dated March 11, 422, and it asserts the primacy of the bishop of Rome in a way that would be reasserted frequently by many successor popes in the first and second millennia. It states,

> We have directed to the synod [of Corinth] . . . such writings that all the brethren may know . . . that there is to be no review of our judgment. In fact, it has never been licit to deliberate again on that which has once been decided by the Apostolic See.[139]

Note that the primacy of Rome is asserted by the claim that no other see has the authority to put into doubt that which the Apostolic See (Rome) has judged. The pope also seems to take it for granted that an Eastern bishop would know the truthfulness of this assertion, since the pope merely asserts this claim without any argumentation or expectation of reservation on the recipient's part.

The same pope also wrote to the Eastern bishops of Thessalonica and equated communion with Rome with communion with the Christian Church. He states,

> It is certain that this [the Roman church] is, as it were, like the head of its members for the churches spread throughout the whole world, and if anyone cuts himself off from her, he is exiled from the Christian religion, since he no longer can share in the same fellowship.[140]

This claim would later be reasserted in the Formula of Hormisdas, signed by over 250 Eastern bishops.

Pope Boniface also wrote to the bishops in Macedonia and said,

> No one has ever boldly raised his hands against the apostolic eminence, from whose judgment it is not permissible to dissent; no one has rebelled against this who did not wish judgment to be passed upon him.[141]

Once more, notice the ease with which the Roman pontiff asserts the papal claim, to a group of Eastern bishops, that the See of Rome is judged by no other see.

So, what should one make of forgeries—like the *Symmachian forgeries*, allegedly (but not really) written by Pope St. Symmachus (498-514), which teach that Rome is judged by no other see? Why would there be a need to create a forgery if Rome already held this doctrine?

Simply put, there *was* something in the tradition undergirding it. Edward Siecienski admits that the teaching in this forgery had been expressed already, authentically, by Pope Gelasius.[142]

So, it would not have been to introduce a new concept. Rather, it would more likely be for the purpose of strengthening an already existent claim. Moreover, there is evidence that this view was in fact held in the time of Symmachus, as an Italian council held in 502 determined that "no human court could judge" the pope.[143]

As for the Donation of Constantine, it is ironic to note that many in the East accepted the document. How could this be unless its claims about papal authority were rooted in some truth? For instance, the Protestant scholar Henry Chadwick notes that "the twelfth-century patriarch of Antioch, Theodore Balsamon, interpreted the Donation of

Constantine as empowering the patriarch of New Rome [Constantinople]."[144]

And, Chadwick notes, at the time of the 1054 controversy, the patriarch of Constantinople, Michael Cerularius (1000-1059), used the Donation of Constantine to bolster the claims of his own see, saying,

> But his ambition for his see is sufficiently attested by Balsamon's report that he interpreted the Donation of Constantine to mean that the supreme authority over the world Church bestowed by the emperor on the Roman bishop was now transferred to Constantine's New Rome.[145]

This shows that in the first millennium, Constantinople did not necessarily deny that the bishop of Rome exercised papal primacy; rather, Constantinople claimed that this power had been transferred from Old Rome (the pope) to New Rome (Constantinople).

The folly of this view is apparent when we consider the claims of indefectibility made by the Roman See. In other words, there would be no need to transfer the authority of the bishop of Rome to another see since the Roman See would never defect from the Faith. Moreover, the patriarch of Constantinople does not claim this kind of authority today, so it is an untenable view for an Orthodox to maintain.

The Donation of Constantine was a forgery; that much is true. But even this forgery shows that the claims of papal authority at the time of its fabrication were rooted in some truth. That is why Constantinople did not immediately dismiss it as a forgery, and why it had any staying power to begin with.

18

"Pope Gregory the Great denied universal jurisdiction"

One of the most common objections Orthodox will make against the papacy is the claim that Pope Gregory the Great denied the Catholic doctrine of universal papal jurisdiction when he rejected the title *universal bishop*, which the patriarch of Constantinople John the Faster (d. 595) used in his day. Orthodox will often point to the following words from one of Gregory's letters:

> Now I confidently say that whosoever calls himself, or desires to be called, Universal Priest, is in his elation the precursor of Antichrist, because he proudly puts himself above all others.[146]

It is certainly true that Gregory wrote the above, but what did he mean? And does it contradict the Catholic claim that the pope is the supreme head of the Church, with universal jurisdiction in the affairs of all the bishops of the world?

Gregory tells us in his letter to Eusebius of Thessalonica (sixth century), "If one, as he supposes, is universal bishop, it remains that you are not bishops."[147]

Certainly, if John the Faster had meant that all other bishops were not actually bishops by the use of the title *universal bishop*, which he did not, then Gregory would have been right to reject it. In fact, Vatican I, which teaches that the pope has a supreme role over the Church, rejects the same thing Gregory rejected:

> This power of the supreme pontiff by no means detracts from that ordinary and immediate power of episcopal jurisdiction, by which bishops, who have succeeded to the place of the apostles by appointment of the Holy Spirit, tend and govern individually the particular flocks which have been assigned to them. On the contrary, this power of theirs is asserted, supported, and defended by the supreme and universal pastor; for St. Gregory the Great says, "My honor is the honor of the whole Church. My honor is the steadfast strength of my brethren. Then do I receive true honor, when it is denied to none of those to whom honor is due."[148]

And so, the same council that defined the supreme and universal role of the pope also rejected, as Gregory did, the title *universal bishop*. However, Vatican I, and Gregory the Great, did not deny the true sense in which the pope plays a universal and supreme role in the Church. This is why Gregory can also say,

> And it is exceedingly doubtful whether he says such things to us sincerely, or in fact because he is being attacked by his fellow bishops: for, as to his saying that he is subject to the Apostolic See, if any fault is found in bishops, I know not what bishop is not subject to it. But when no fault requires it to be otherwise, all according to the principle of humility are equal.[149]

Clearly, Orthodox who use the words of Gregory to mean he rejected the papal claims defined by Vatican I are guilty of equivocating between what Gregory condemned as a "universal bishop" with what Vatican I affirmed about the "universal pastor." Moreover, Gregory the Great threatened to annul any decision made by the East to assert the title of universal bishop for the patriarch of Constantinople—an act that would make little sense if the pope believed he did not have jurisdiction over Eastern affairs.[150] This, in part, is why Orthodox scholar Edward Siescienski can say of Gregory,

> Gregory thus provides modern ecumenical discussion on the papacy with a two-edged sword, for on one hand there is no doubt that he defended the primacy of Rome vigorously and grounded this pre-eminence on his see's Petrine origin rather than any conciliar decision.[151]

This is also why the Protestant historian Philip Schaff can say Gregory exercised authority over the Eastern churches.[152]

In another nod to the pope's universal jurisdiction, Gregory describes the annulling of a synod held in Constantinople by his predecessor, Pope Pelagius II (579-590). He states:

> Now eight years ago, in the time of my predecessor of holy memory Pelagius, our brother and fellow bishop John in the city of Constantinople, seeking occasion from another cause, held a synod in which he attempted to call himself universal bishop. Which as soon as my said predecessor knew, he dispatched letters annulling by the authority of the holy apostle Peter the acts of the said synod; of which letters I have taken care to send copies to Your Holiness.[153]

Consequently, rather than being a witness against Catholic ecclesiology, Gregory the Great is one of its star witnesses!

19

"Rome's primacy in the early Church was not because of a divine institution"

Orthodox tend to argue that the pope's primacy and authority in the early Church were due to the bishop of Rome being the bishop of the most prominent city in the Roman empire. They also claim Rome's primacy was the result of its many martyrs and faithful bishops. So, for Orthodox, the papacy's primacy is not due to a divine institution, but is the result of historical factors and is thus transferrable to a bishop of a different territory.

Catholics recognize that the pope's image in the early Church was bolstered by Rome's many martyrs and faithful bishops. The Church also grants that the pope's image was magnified because he was the bishop of the most prominent city in the Roman Empire. However, Catholics also claim that the pope's primacy and authority are due to Christ having made St. Peter the head of the apostolic college, and this role of leadership passes to the successor of Peter—that is, the pope. Thus, for Catholics, the papacy and its primacy are divine institutions and the other factors merely bolstered and developed their prominence in time. Consequently, the primacy of the pope cannot fail or be transferred to the territory of another bishop.

It won't take long for a Catholic discerning Eastern Ortho-doxy to encounter Orthodox who deny the divine origin of the papacy and attribute its primacy in the early Church to other factors. Some of the common reasons are summed up by Fr. John Meyendorff as follows:

> Already before Nicaea, the Church at Rome enjoyed a special prestige in the Christian world. . . . It was not a question of one church having "power" over the others, but of a real "authority" justified not only by the fact that the church of Rome was founded by the apostles, but also by its seniority, its numerical importance, and the incomparable prestige of the capital. None of these elements in itself was enough to give the bishop of Rome special authority, but altogether they gave him a quite exceptional position.[154]

Essentially, Meyendorff says Rome's primacy can be ex-plained by its apostolic succession, "numerical significance," (be it the size of the city's population or the number of saints it produced in its early history), and prominence in the Ro-man Empire.

It is important to highlight the claim about Rome's status in the empire, because it touches on a phenomenon found in the first millennium, which Fr. Francis Dvornik calls *the principle of accommodation.*[155] This principle describes the phe-nomenon, going back to apostolic times, where the churches located in cities that were prominent in the Roman Empire were held in higher esteem than less prominent cities. The Church would thus adapt its ecclesial structure to the fluc-tuating structure of the empire.

Some Orthodox argue that the principle of accommoda-tion shows that the church of Rome was held in the highest esteem because it was considered the most esteemed city in the Roman Empire. Catholics, on the other hand, may grant some truth to the principle of accommodation but will also say Rome's position in the early Church was due to its relation to Peter. This debate between East and West is at the heart of the schism, according to some Orthodox.[156]

Perhaps you can see where this is going: if Rome was primary because of its position in the Roman Empire, then surely the primacy that Rome enjoyed should be transferred to any see whose greatness should overtake Rome. And which city must immediately come to mind?

As Meyendorff puts it,

> This priority given to *Constantinople* could not be regarded by contemporaries as a caesaropapist revolution, as Roman Catholic historians later asserted. It showed only that it was possible for *any church* to play a primary role in Christendom, provided that the other churches recognized that its authority was justified.[157]

Orthodox like Meyendorff will use this argument and then cite canon three of the First Council of Constantinople and canon twenty-eight of the Council of Chalcedon as proof that the primacy of Old Rome (Rome) was transferred to New Rome (Constantinople).

Clearly, Orthodox who make this argument attribute Rome's primacy in the early Church to factors other than a divine relationship with Peter, the first pope. However, this was not always the case with the East. Edward Siecienski notes, "Meyendorff himself admits that part of the difficulty is that, at different times and for different reasons, East and West seemed to accept both principles."[158]

In other words, Orthodox have a serious challenge in reconciling their current view about Roman primacy when some in the East did not limit themselves to the principle of accommodation, but also held to Rome's primacy because of Rome's unique claim to Peter.

However, Catholics should recognize that there is some truth to the principle of accommodation and that it played a role in bolstering and developing the status of the church of Rome. It may also be conceded that Rome's numerical status, apostolic succession, and numerous martyrs also were factors in its prominence in the early Church. However, were these the only reasons for its primacy?

Many popes who are saints in Eastern Orthodoxy, along with some of the ecumenical councils, recognized that the papacy also has primacy based on the words of Jesus to Peter in Matthew 16:18–19. For example, note what the Council of Rome, led by Pope St. Damasus I (366-384), claimed in 382 about Rome's primacy:

> Yet the holy Roman church has been set before the rest by no conciliar decrees, but has obtained the primacy by the voice of our Lord and Savior in the Gospel: "Thou are Peter and upon this rock . . . shall be loosed in heaven."
> . . . The first see of the apostle Peter is therefore the Roman church, "not having spot or wrinkle or any such thing."[159]

This is a difficulty for Eastern Orthodox, because Damasus is a saint in Orthodoxy. At this juncture, Orthodox have to explain why some of their saints in the first millennium held to what Orthodox would later consider to be heretical. Additionally, what was said by Damasus was effectively repeated by Philip, the Roman legate at the Council of Ephesus:

There is no doubt and in fact it has been known in all ages, that the holy and most blessed Peter, prince and head of the apostles, pillar of the Faith, and foundation of the Catholic Church, received the keys of the kingdom from our Lord Jesus Christ the Savior and Redeemer of the human race, and that to him was given the power of loosing and binding sins: who down even to today and forever both lives and judges in his successors. The holy and most blessed pope Celestine, according to due order, is his successor and holds his place, and us he sent to supply his place in this holy synod, which the most humane and Christian emperors have commanded to assemble, bearing in mind and continually watching over the Catholic faith.[160]

Later, Pope St. Leo the Great would echo this teaching:

For although the pastors, each one singly, preside over their own flocks with a special care and know that they will have to render an account for the sheep entrusted to them, we have a duty which is shared with all; in fact the function of each one is a part of our work: so that when men resort to the see of the blessed apostle Peter from the whole world, and seek from our stewardship that love of the whole Church entrusted to him by the Lord, the greater our duty to the whole, the heavier we feel the burden to rest on us.

There is a further reason for our celebration: not only the apostolic but also the episcopal dignity of the most blessed Peter, who does not cease to preside over his see and obtains an abiding partnership with the eternal Priest. For the stability which the rock himself was given by that Rock, Christ, he conveyed also to his successors, and wheresoever any steadfastness is apparent, there without doubt is to be seen the strength of the shepherd.[161]

The Formula of Hormisdas, signed by the Eastern bishops to end the Acacian Schism, repeats this concept:

The beginning of salvation is to preserve the rule of a correct faith and to deviate in no respect from the constitutions of the Fathers. And because the teaching of our Lord Jesus Christ cannot be allowed to fail, who said, "Thou art Peter, and upon this rock I will build my Church," etc., these things which were said are proved by the effects of things, because in the Apostolic See religion has always been preserved without spot or blemish.[162]

This is why Orthodox priest and author Fr. Laurent Cleenewerck concedes,

Since the times of Stephen, the Roman church has consistently taught that her bishop is the successor of Peter in a unique sense and that he holds by divine right a primacy of power over the universal Church. In other words, Rome made no secret that her ecclesiology and concept of primacy were different from that of the East. . . . This was expressed consistently and unambiguously by a number of popes commemorated as saints in the Orthodox Church, including such luminaries as Leo, Agatho, and Hadrian. As we have seen, this ecclesiology was accepted by a number of Eastern saints.[163]

Pope St. Gelasius I (492-496), a saint in Eastern Orthodoxy, repeated the judgment of Pope Damasus I and laughed at the idea that Constantinople should be second among the churches based on its position in the empire.[164] He even questioned the logic of this argumentation, since emperors have lived in Trier, and yet the bishop of this territory does not claim a high rank among the bishops. Moreover, for Gelasius, Rome's position among the churches was because of a divine commission, not because of its status in the empire or a generic claim to apostolic succession.

This is also why Catholic priest, scholar, and historian Fr. Richard Price, having analyzed the documents of antiquity, comfortably asserts that "The bishops of Rome, since ancient times also called *papa* or pope, claimed a primacy over the Church that derived from Christ's commission to Peter."[165]

Similar to Gelasius, St. Maximus the Confessor, a saint highly venerated in Eastern Orthodoxy, asserts that Rome's position among the churches is because of a divine institution, not just because of conciliar decrees or Rome's status in the empire. He states,

> Let him [i.e., Pyrrhus] hasten before all things to satisfy the Roman See, for if it is satisfied, all will agree in calling him pious and orthodox. [For h]e is only wasting words who thinks he must convince or lure such people as myself, instead of satisfying or entreating the blessed pope of the most holy catholic church of Rome, i.e., the Apostolic Throne, which is from the incarnate Son himself and which, in accordance with the holy canons and the definitions of faith, received from all the holy councils universal and supreme dominion, authority, and the power over all God's churches throughout the world to bind and loose.[166]

Elsewhere, he adds,

How much more in the case of the clergy and church of the Romans, which from of old until now, as the elder of all the churches which are under the sun, presides over all? Having surely received this canonically, as well from councils and the apostles, as from the princes of the latter, and being numbered in their company, she is subject to no writings or issues of synodical documents, on account of the eminence of her pontificate, even as in all these things all are equally subject to her according to sacerdotal law.[167]

Another witness to this perspective may be seen in Pope Hadrian (772-795)'s letter to the emperors Constantine and Irene, read out loud at the seventh ecumenical council (787), which repeats the claim that the papacy is a divine institution:

Stand firm; for if you abide with perseverance in the orthodox Faith in which you have begun and so through you the sacred and venerable images are restored in those regions to their former state—just as the lord and emperor Constantine of pious memory and blessed Helena, who promulgated the orthodox Faith, raised up the holy, catholic, and apostolic church of Rome as your spiritual mother, and with the other orthodox emperors venerated it as the head of all the churches. . . .

[And i]f, moreover, following the traditions of the orthodox faith, you embrace the judgment of the church of the blessed Peter prince of the apostles and, as the holy emperors your predecessors did of old, so you too venerate it with honor and love his vicar from the depths of your hearts, or rather if your rule granted by God follows their orthodox faith in accordance with our holy Roman church, the prince of the apostles, to whom was given by the Lord God the power to bind and to loose sins in heaven and on earth.[168]

It continues,

> For sacred authority reveals the marks of his [Peter's] dig-
> nity and how veneration should be paid to his supreme
> see by all the faithful throughout the world. For the Lord
> appointed him, as key-bearer of the kingdom of heaven,
> to be prince over all, and honors him with the privilege
> by which the keys of the kingdom of heaven were en-
> trusted to him. . . .
>
> For the blessed Peter prince of the apostles, who was
> the first to preside over the Apostolic See, left the pri-
> macy of his apostolate and pastoral responsibility to his
> successors, who are to sit in his most sacred see forever.
> The power of authority, as it had been granted to him by
> the Lord God our Savior, he in his turn conferred and
> transmitted by divine command to the pontiffs who suc-
> ceeded him, in whose tradition we venerate the sacred
> effigy of Christ and the images of his holy mother, the
> apostles, and all the saints.[169]

Some may object to the citation above on the basis that the
Greek version mitigates some of the papal claims. However,
Richard Price rightly notes that the above translation is based
on the authentic version read out at the council.[170] Also, the
Greek version, which is likely a later alteration to the text,[171]
shows that the East was aware that the papacy had claimed at
an ecumenical council that it was a divine institution. Since
the fathers of the council received the letter by Hadrian without protest, it shows that they were aware that they were in
communion with a pope who maintained the papal claims.

If the papal claims are heretical, as many Orthodox today
claim, this means that the council fathers were knowingly
in communion with heretics. It also reflects poorly on the

East to resort to altering papal documents to mitigate papal claims, which, despite the alterations, may still be found in substance in the Greek version.

Seemingly oblivious to what was actually read at Nicaea II, the Orthodox polemicist Abbé Guettée attempts to wave away the Catholic position:

> The acts of the seventh ecumenical council, like those of the preceding ones, clearly prove that the bishop of Rome was only first *in honor* in the Church; that his testimony had no doctrinal weight, except in so far as it might be regarded as that of the Western Church; that there was yet no *individual* authority in the Church, but a *collective authority* only, of which the sacerdotal body was the echo and interpreter.[172]

Unfortunately, this kind of poor engagement with the primary sources of the councils is all too common among Orthodox polemicists. For better or worse, numerous other primary sources from popes, saints, and councils can be presented to show that the papacy's primacy in the first millennium rested on the claim to a divine institution. Moreover, plenty of other secondary sources from Catholic, Orthodox, and Protestant scholars can be marshaled to demonstrate that there was a strong contingent of Western and Eastern figures who maintained that Rome's primacy is based primarily on a divine institution.

Some may ask: What do Catholics make of canon three of Constantinople I and canon twenty-eight of Chalcedon, which seem to suggest that Rome's primacy was based on its position in the Roman Empire?

First, the third canon of Constantinople I was not accepted by the bishop of Rome in the fourth century. Moreover, one year after the council attempted to push through canon three at Constantinople I, Damasus (as seen above) stated that Rome's primacy is not primarily due to "conciliar de-crees." Canon three failed, so others at the Council of Chal-cedon tried to push the same sentiment forward once more with canon twenty-eight. However, Pope Leo, solemnly invoking the authority of Peter, nullified that canon as well. The bishop of Constantinople and the emperor acquiesced to Rome's decision, though Emperor Justinian adopted the canon in Roman law through *Novella* 131 (the *Novella* being a Roman legal constitution) a century later.[173]

Eventually, Constantinople did prevail—to a point. As late as Pope Nicholas I (800-867), Rome spoke of Alex-andria having priority before Constantinople,[174] but Rome eventually accepted the twenty-eighth canon of Constanti-nople in an implicit way, in 869-870, in canon twenty-one of the Fourth Council of Constantinople, and again in the Fourth Lateran Council in 1215, an ecumenical council by Catholic standards. According to Lateran IV,

> Renewing the ancient privileges of the patriarchal sees, we decree, with the approval of this sacred universal synod, that after the Roman church, which through the Lord's disposition has a primacy of ordinary power over all other churches inasmuch as it is the mother and mistress of all Christ's faithful, the church of Constantinople shall have the first place, the church of Alexandria the second place, the church of Antioch the third place, and the church of Je-rusalem the fourth place, each maintaining its own rank.[175]

So, did Rome concede that its primacy had been trans-ferred to Constantinople? Certainly not. Just because Rome accepted Constantinople as being second in prominence, taking priority over Alexandria, Antioch, and Jerusalem, that does not mean that Rome's primacy was based solely on

Rome's status in the empire. In fact, Pope St. Agatho's letter, read and accepted at the Third Council of Constantinople, implicitly denies such a possibility:

> For this is the rule of the true Faith, which this spiritual mother of your most tranquil empire, the apostolic Church of Christ, has both in prosperity and in adversity always held and defended with energy; which, it will be proved, by the grace of Almighty God, has never erred from the path of the apostolic Tradition, nor has she been depraved by yielding to heretical innovations, but from the beginning she has received the Christian faith from her founders, the princes of the apostles of Christ, and remains undefiled unto the end, according to the divine promise of the Lord and Savior himself, which he uttered in the holy Gospels to the prince of his disciples: saying, Peter, Peter, behold, Satan has desired to have you, that he might sift you as wheat; but I have prayed for you, that [your] faith fail not. And when you are converted, strengthen your brethren.[176]

Note that Agatho claims that Rome's indefectibility in its teaching office is rooted in Christ's promise to preserve the faith of Peter. Thus, if Rome will never defect from the Faith because of a divine promise, it has no need to transfer its primacy elsewhere.

It should also be stressed that Constantinople today does not claim to have such authority as expressed by Agatho, so it would be unreasonable to maintain that the See of Constantinople has such authority when its occupant does not claim such an authority for himself. Moreover, Orthodox consider such ecclesiology to be heretical, so if the See of Constantinople does have an element of indefectibility to its teaching office, then the Orthodox, including Constantinople, deem as heretical something that they actually possess—which seems to immediately disprove such a claim to indefectibility.

In summary, it should not be denied that Rome's primacy in the early Church was bolstered by political factors, along with its many saints, its martyrs, and its apostolic foundation. Yet Eastern and Western acknowledgments of its primacy, as especially rooted in a divine institution, cannot be denied, nor can we believe that this primacy was transferred elsewhere.

20

"The pope was merely a first among equals in the first millennium"

Orthodox are divided on some aspects of the pope's authority. Some claim he is merely the "first among equals" and claim that this means he is to be given the most respect, and may have a few liturgical privileges, but this primacy never translates into anything more. Other Orthodox are willing to concede that the role of the pope may include a certain moral authority, and his consent may even be necessary for settling doctrines that pertain to the universal Church, but they would say he does not possess a coercive authority that is able to bind consciences or interfere in the affairs of another bishop.

Catholics believe that the pope is entrusted with the care of the universal Church. He may bind consciences in doctrinal matters and intervene in the internal affairs of another bishop. Additionally, his ratification is absolutely necessary for any definitive decision on the part of the college of bishops acting in an ecumenical council.

Some Orthodox object to the Catholic view of papal primacy by claiming that the pope was considered merely a "first among equals" in the first millennium.

One problem here is that the Orthodox do not have a unified view on what "first among equals" actually means. This is why the Orthodox canonist and scholar Fr. John H. Erickson can say,

> While the patriarch of Constantinople is acknowledged by all as "first among equals," what this priority involves in the actual life of the Orthodox churches in our day is by no means clear."[177]

Also, the evidence shows that the pope was more than a first among equals, as in the case of Pope St. Martin I (venerated as a saint in Orthodoxy), who in the seventh century intervened in the affairs of the territories of Antioch and Jerusalem during the Monothelite crisis. The Anglican convert to Catholicism Thomas William Allies (1813-1903) described the situation:

> About the year 650, Pope St. Martin exercises his power of universal jurisdiction by constituting John, bishop of Philadelphia, his vicar in the East, "that you may correct the things which are wanting, and appoint bishops, presbyters, and deacons in every city of those which are subject to the see both of Jerusalem and of Antioch; we charge you to do this in every way, in virtue of the apostolic authority which was given us by the Lord in the person of most holy Peter, prince of the apostles; on account of the necessities of our time, and the pressure of the nations."[178]

This kind of intervention in the affairs of an Eastern jurisdiction is also seen in Martin's predecessor, Pope St. Theodore I (642-649), who is also venerated as a saint in

Orthodoxy, who commissioned the Eastern bishop Stephen of Dor to depose heretical bishops in the Patriarchate of Jerusalem. Stephen recounts at the Lateran Synod of 649,

> This fact I communicated earlier to the Apostolic See, namely to the sainted pope Theodore; he by an apostolic letter appointed me his representative, despite my unworthiness, and by an all-sacred instruction bade me, apart from conducting other ecclesiastical business, to carry out a canonical deposition of the bishops ordained in this way, if they proved incorrigible. This indeed I did, particularly in view of the fact that of their own accord they had deserted the truth for error.[179]

How can popes who are merely first among equals appoint bishops, presbyters, and deacons in the territory of Eastern patriarchates and appoint other bishops to depose heretical bishops in Eastern jurisdictions? Could the patriarch of Constantinople, the first among equals in Orthodoxy today (at least for the Eastern Orthodox who are still in communion with him), appoint bishops, presbyters, and deacons in the territory of Antioch and Jerusalem if he deemed it necessary? Could he appoint a bishop to depose heretical bishops in other patriarchates? Most Orthodox would shudder to think such a thing.

Yet the popes exercised this authority because they maintained that they were empowered to do so by Christ.

Another example that shows that the pope was more than a first among equals can be seen in a letter to Theodore I by the Eastern metropolitan of Cyprus:

> To the most blessed father of fathers, archbishop and universal patriarch, Theodore, Sergius, the humble bishop,

health in the Lord. Christ our God hath established thy Apostolic See, O Sacred Head, as a divinely-fixed immovable foundation, whereon the Faith is brightly inscribed. For "thou art Peter," as the divine Word truly pronounced, and on thy foundation the pillars of the Church are fixed. Into thy hands he put the keys of the heavens, and pronounced that thou shouldest bind and loose in earth and heaven with power."[180]

This clearly demonstrates the existence of the universal jurisdiction of the pope in the seventh century.

Can Orthodox today say the first among equals is a "divinely-fixed immovable foundation," considering that they believe that the position of first has passed from Rome to Constantinople? Would the Patriarchate of Moscow, currently not in communion with Constantinople, claim this of either Rome or Constantinople? There seems to be some discontinuity between the primacy as expressed in this first-millennium source and Eastern Orthodoxy today.

It should also be noted that the case of Pope Leo the Great annulling a decision of an ecumenical council (see Objection 16) shows that the pope held more than a mere primacy of honor, since it demonstrates that he exercised real authority over a canon passed by Eastern bishops assembled in an ecumenical council. Can the first among equals in Orthodoxy do such a thing today? Most Orthodox would answer in the negative. Thus, it is inaccurate to compare the concept of the first among equals in Orthodoxy today to the position of the pope in the first millennium.

21

"Rome, Alexandria, and Antioch were all considered Petrine sees and thus equal in authority"

One argument that is sure to rattle the cage of a Catholic inquirer into Orthodoxy is the "three Petrine sees" claim. Those who use this argument say that Pope Gregory the Great taught that the sees of Rome, Alexandria, and Antioch are one see, since they were all established by St. Peter. They base this on the words of St. Gregory to Eulogius, the bishop of Alexandria:

> Wherefore though there are many apostles, yet with regard to the principality itself the see of the prince of the apostles alone has grown strong in authority, which in three places is the see of one.[181]

From this they assume that Gregory meant that all three of these sees are equal in authority. For instance, Abbé Guettée says,

> And no wonder; for he did not regard the See of Rome as the only see of St. Peter. He expressly acknowledged that the sees of Alexandria and Antioch were, quite as much as

that of Rome, the see of the first of the apostles, and that these three sees were but one.[182]

Catholics agree with Gregory that the sees of Alexandria and Antioch are sees established by Peter. For example, the Catholic priest and scholar Dom John Chapman happily admits this, saying, "The Western Fathers see three Petrine sees" . . . but, he goes on, "of which one has inherited all St. Peter's primacy, while the other two have a reflection of it."[183]

And so, we can see that Catholics do not conclude that the sees of Antioch and Alexandria are not subject to the bishop of Rome. In fact, Gregory the Great himself would not have said the sees of Alexandria and Antioch are exempt from Rome's power, despite, *prima facie*, the quote referenced by Abbé Guettée above. For example, recall our response to objection 18, in which we mentioned Gregory's remark to John, bishop of Syracuse, that "if any fault is found in bishops, I know not what bishop is not subject to [the Apostolic See]."[184]

In other words, during times when there is no dispute between or among the churches, all bishops are equal. During such times, we can even emphasize the special unity that Rome, Alexandria, and Antioch share as sees established by Peter. However, per Gregory, during times of dispute, even the other Petrine sees would be subject to Rome.

Think of it like this. Three brothers may share a special solidarity due to sharing the same parents, but when push comes to shove, they may not always be in agreement. In such cases, there could be a brother, usually the oldest, who, by virtue of his seniority over the other two, makes the final decision. Likewise, Rome, Alexandria, and Antioch may share a common heritage, but when the rubber meets the road, Rome has seniority (and authority) over the other two sees.

It should be noted that in reality, the Alexandrian see was not always "equal" to the Roman even per a more relaxed understanding of equality. For example, St. Cyril, the patriarch of Alexandria, submitted himself to the bishop of Rome in matters of orthodoxy. On one occasion, Cyril wrote to Pope Celestine with regard to the heretic Nestorius:

> We shall not publicly withdraw from communion with him until we have shared this matter with your religiousness. Therefore, be so good as to decree what you think right, and whether one ought to be in communion with him or rather issue a public refusal on the grounds that no one can be in communion with one who holds and teaches such things.[185]

Note that Cyril asks Celestine whether or not he should be in communion with Nestorius and whether Nestorius teaches orthodox theology or heterodoxy. Clearly, the See of Alexandria was subject to the See of Rome in this instance, and Gregory the Great would likely have been aware of this.

One final proof that Gregory believed that the bishop of Rome has a unique claim to the authority of Peter may be found in his letter to Eusebius of Thessalonica, where he says,

> For if any one, as we do not believe will be the case, should disregard in any part this present writing, let him know that he is segregated from the peace of the blessed Peter, the prince of the apostles.[186]

Notice that the pope here claims that those who disregard his letter will be cut off from fellowship with Peter.

He is not under the impression that he must first verify the content of his letter with Alexandria and Antioch before he can say anyone is cut off. Thus, it is unnatural to read Pope Gregory's comments about the three Petrine sees in any way that contradicts his obvious recognition elsewhere that the bishop of Rome is a unique successor to Peter—in a way that the other bishops, including those of Alexandria and Antioch, are not.

Additionally, when Dioscorus of Alexandria (d. 454) attempted to anathematize Pope St. Leo the Great, the Council of Chalcedon condemned him in the following words:

> But he has greatly surpassed his first crimes with his later ones, and had the presumption to pronounce excommunication against the most holy and sacred Leo archbishop of Great Rome.[187]

This is certainly an odd thing to do if the Eastern council fathers considered Alexandria to be on equal footing with Rome. Orthodox who employ this argument seem to be out of step with their own ecumenical council.

In summary, Gregory the Great's comments emphasizing the solidarity among the three Petrine sees should not be taken too strictly, because that would contradict his view, stated elsewhere, about the primacy of the bishop of Rome. Also, this argument is not sustainable, since there are many instances of Rome exercising authority over Alexandria and Antioch. Lastly, there aren't any Orthodox bishops today, to my knowledge, who maintain the view that Rome, Alexandria, and Antioch share the primacy of Peter in a unique way. Rather, it is more common to find the position that the bishop of Constantinople precedes Alexandria and Antioch, based on canon twenty-eight of the Council of Chalcedon.

In other words, some Orthodox may use the "three Petrine sees" argument to undermine the papacy, but this view is not consistent with modern Eastern Orthodox ecclesiology, nor do many—if any—Orthodox hierarchs share it.

22

"The Catholic Church accepted Constantinople IV's rule against the *filioque*"

An argument that has found fame among online Orthodox is that Rome accepted a council that forbade the addition of the *filioque* into the Nicene Creed. For instance, Orthodox priest and author Fr. Andrew Stephen Damick claims that "Pope John VIII in the ninth century condemned the addition of the *filioque* to the Nicene Creed, but he was overruled by his successors in the eleventh century."[188]

Though it is not explicitly stated, this is most likely a reference to Pope John VIII (872-882)'s alleged acceptance of the Council of Constantinople 879-880, which forbade additions to the Creed in certain cases.

Many Catholics who look into Eastern Orthodoxy have their faith shaken when they hear Orthodox claim that a pope signed off on an ecumenical council that forbade the insertion of the *filioque*! How can this be?

First, let's look at the council in question. Was Constantinople 879-880 truly an ecumenical council?

Catholics and Orthodox agree that ecumenical councils are authoritative on a universal level, but there is a difference on what constitutes an ecumenical council. Even the

Orthodox are divided on the question: some Orthodox accept Constantinople 879-880 as ecumenical, whereas others downgrade it as less authoritative.

The difference is due to the criteria used to determine what constitutes an ecumenical council. Are they merely councils that the emperor calls? If so, then the Council of Ephesus 449 would need to be considered one. However, Orthodox reject Ephesus 449 as a council that deviates from the Faith.

Others may say that acceptance by the five major centers of Christianity (Rome, Alexandria, Antioch, Constantinople, and Jerusalem) is what determines an ecumenical council. However, if this were the case, it would mean that the reunion Council of Florence (1431-1449) is ecumenical. Yet Orthodox reject this council, too, as a departure from the Faith.

Others argue that an ecumenical council is a council that has been received by the Orthodox churches as universally authoritative. This is problematic because many of the ecumenical councils in the first millennium that the Orthodox accept were considered authoritative before their universal acceptance. It also begs the question: Received by whom? Some churches did not accept Ephesus (431) or Chalcedon (451). So this theory of reception already assumes which churches maintain orthodox theology when ecumenical councils are often necessary to determine what is orthodox theology. This produces a vicious circle and proves to be an inadequate answer to the question of what makes a council ecumenical.

Catholics, on the other hand, say that an ecumenical council is a universally binding council and is determined by papal ratification. In other words, if the pope ratifies the council as *universally* binding in scope, then it is an ecumenical council. So, for Catholics, an ecumenical council cannot be held without, at the very least, the ratification of a pope either during or after the council.

Did the pope sign off on forbidding the insertion of the *filioque* clause into the Creed? Not exactly.

To reiterate, the council in question above is the Council of Constantinople 879-880. The relevant clause from the council states,

> Thus, having in mind and declaring all these things, we embrace with mind and tongue (τῇ διανοίᾳ καὶ γλώσσῃ) and declare to all people with a loud voice the *Horos* [Rule—that is, a rule of faith] of the most pure faith of the Christians that has come down to us from above through the Fathers, subtracting nothing, adding nothing, falsifying nothing; for subtraction and addition, when no heresy is stirred up by the ingenious fabrications of the evil one, introduce disapprobation of those who are exempt from blame and an inexcusable assault on the Fathers. As for the act of changing with falsified words the *Horoi* [rules, boundaries] of the Fathers is much worse than the previous one.[189]

Note that the rule forbids any addition or subtraction to the Creed with "falsified words," or any alteration to the Creed, unless a heresy is stirred up by the devil. In the case of the *filioque* clause, the doctrine is not false, and it is well known that the *filioque* was inserted into the Creed in Spain in order to combat the heresy of Arianism—the heresy that Jesus is not fully divine. Professing that the Holy Spirit proceeds from the Father and the Son emphasizes the Son's divinity. As the *filioque* was used to combat Spanish Arianism, it meets the exception the council granted.

As far as papal acceptance of this rule, there is a long and convoluted history behind John VIII (the pope at the time) and this council. Yet let's grant for the moment that the pope accepted Constantinople 879-880. Even if the insertion of the *filioque* into the Creed *did* violate the rule proposed by the council—though, as we established above, it doesn't—the rule forbidding additions to the Creed is a disciplinary rule, not a dogma, and so the pope, or a future pope, could reverse it, and the Latin-rite Church would then be able to insert the *filioque* into its liturgical recitation of the Creed.

Lastly, recall that Constantinople 879-880 was mostly a disciplinary council, so it would be fine for the pope to discontinue or reverse certain disciplines (not any dogmas or definitive teachings) therein. This would not constitute a change in the Faith. Contrast this with a council like Nicaea I (325): if the pope dispensed with the Nicaean provision that the Son is eternally begotten of the Father, that would be a problem! But Constantinople 879-880 didn't have anything like that.

23

"The Council of Ephesus forbade alterations to the Creed"

If Constantinople 879-880 won't work, Orthodox might reason, then surely the Council of Ephesus (431) will do the trick. Allegedly, Ephesus also forbade any alterations to the Creed.

Mark of Ephesus (1392-1444), the leading Orthodox figure at the reunion Council of Florence, claimed that this addition is "the original reason for the schism."[190] In fact, Mark's argument against the Catholic position heavily relied on the claim that the *filioque* clause is against the Council of Ephesus, so this is by no means a new argument in Orthodox apologetics circles.[191]

Unfortunately for Mark, and the Orthodox who use this argument, not only did the Council of Ephesus not forbid all alterations to the Creed, but the historical context of Ephesus backfires on the Orthodox who make the claim. Let's consider both of these points.

What did the Council of Ephesus say about alterations to the Creed? Here are the words of the seventh canon at the council:

No one is allowed to produce or write or compose another creed beside the one laid down with [the aid of] the Holy Spirit by the holy fathers assembled at Nicaea.[192]

Notice that the council did not say that "any alteration" to the Creed is forbidden. Rather, it is forbidden to produce "another creed." In other words, this is a prohibition against those who would produce a different creed to be used in opposition to the Nicene Creed. That was certainly the historical context, since this canon was aimed against local Nestorian creeds, which contradicted the faith of the Creed of the Nicene fathers.[193]

Another point to consider is that the Orthodox who use this argument condemn themselves. After all, the Creed that Catholics *and Orthodox* recite in the liturgy is actually the Niceno-*Constantinopolitan* Creed, which significantly varies from the original Creed of Nicaea proposed by the fathers at the Council of Ephesus.[194] For instance, the Nicene Creed proposed by Ephesus has the phrase "both those in heaven and those on earth," which is missing in our Niceno-Constantinopolitan Creed.[195] Additionally, there is a long section condemning the Arians that has been removed from the original Nicene Creed:

> Those who say, "There was when he was not," and "Before being begotten he was not," and that he came into being from things that are not, or assert that the Son of God is from another *hypostasis* or substance or is changeable or alterable, these the catholic and apostolic Church anathematizes.

Clearly, neither Catholics nor Orthodox use the creed proposed by the Council of Nicaea and the fathers of the Council of Ephesus. However, our Niceno-Constantinopolitan Creed is not "another creed" used in opposition to the Nicene Creed. Likewise, the *filioque* clause is not another creed, but is an additive clause used to clarify the faith of the Nicene fathers.

If an Orthodox considers adding one word to the Creed to be "another creed," then wouldn't removing large chunks of the original Nicene Creed also qualify as "another creed"? If an Orthodox were to retort, "But the *filioque* clause is heretical, so it corrupts the Creed," then the Orthodox condemn themselves for being in communion with the Western Church, which taught the *filioque*. As Orthodox author Edward Siecienski notes, "by the late sixth century the *filioque* achieved a level of acceptance in the West bordering on unanimity."[196]

As noted above, Mark of Ephesus called the *filioque* the main reason for the schism between Catholics and Orthodox. Since it was not actually forbidden to add the *filioque* clause to the Creed, nor is the doctrine of the *filioque* heretical, the Orthodox have little reason to use this issue to perpetuate division between themselves and Catholics.

24

"Indulgences are an innovation of the second millennium"

Sooner or later, in one way or another, a Catholic discerning Eastern Orthodoxy will find a wide range of arguments from the Orthodox against the Catholic practice of indulgences.

What are indulgences? Simply put,

> An indulgence is a remission before God of the temporal punishment due to sins whose guilt has already been forgiven, which the faithful Christian who is duly disposed gains under certain prescribed conditions through the action of the Church which, as the minister of redemption, dispenses and applies with authority the treasury of the satisfactions of Christ and the saints (CCC 1471).

Indulgences do not concern the eternal guilt (damnation) due to the commission of a serious sin. Rather, they constitute a remission of the temporal guilt (the temporal effects) of sin—the bad consequences of our sins on earth.

We can see how temporal consequences remain even after eternal consequences are remitted. For instance, if someone steals twenty dollars from a homeless person, but later earnestly confesses this sin, God will forgive him, which includes taking away the eternal consequences of the theft. But the temporal problem remains: a homeless person has been deprived of a necessary means of survival. So, though the sinner may be forgiven by God, he still has the penitential duty to make up for the damage he caused the homeless person. This may take place in the form of restoring the twenty dollars to the homeless person, if this is still possible. If not, a comparable penance may be performed, such as giving twenty dollars to charity.

Similar to the sin above, other sins bring with them temporal consequences. When a person has not fully taken care of the temporal consequences of a sin on his own, an indulgence is one way the Church offers help.

Some Orthodox may reject the validity of indulgences because they reject the concept of temporal punishment. Others may dispute them on the basis that they necessitate selling the forgiveness of sins. Frankly, there are too many arguments from Orthodox against indulgences to address here. For this reason, it may be helpful to address one of the most popular arguments, which is the claim that indulgences are a Catholic innovation of the second millennium.

In a sense, this claim is true! Catholic priest and theologian Ludwig Ott concedes this, saying, "The modern form of indulgence developed in the eleventh century."[197]

However, it does have biblical and first-millennium roots. Indulgences are intimately connected to the concept of temporal punishment, which is rooted in several biblical passages, including 2 Samuel 12:13–14. Indulgences are also tied to other biblical concepts, such as the power of binding and loosing (see CCC 1478), the communion of saints (see CCC 1479), and reconciliation with God and the Church (see CCC 1445). The third century saw the introduction of the practice of reducing a sinner's penitential period through the intercession of the martyrs.[198] These things gave rise to indulgences in the second millennium.

In other words, the practice of issuing indulgences is from the early second millennium, but it is rooted in concepts from the first. Does this pose a problem for Catholicism? No more than the liturgical veneration of icons (most likely not a first-century practice) and the third-century reduction of penitential practices pose for Orthodox. After all, why is the second millennium a standard for practices that are out of bounds? Wouldn't this standard mean that no practice that originates in the second millennium could be used in Orthodoxy? If it's just a matter of forbidding "innovations," then why not say that practices that arose in the third century or the sixth century are also out of bounds as "new" relative to the time of the apostles? There are certainly some Protestants who make such a claim, but Orthodox would not agree. Yet on what basis? It would seem that if we concede that the post-apostolic Church has the authority to introduce new practices in the third century, then it certainly has that authority in the second millennium as well.

Some will say that it might be fine if indulgences were merely practiced by Catholics, but it is unacceptable for the Catholic Church to dogmatize the concept. It is true that the Catholic Church dogmatized indulgences—and this is similar to the Orthodox practice of the liturgical veneration of icons, which was seemingly unknown in the early centuries of the Church. Yet Nicaea II dogmatized the veneration of icons, both for Catholics and for Orthodox. Why? Because the doctrinal concepts that would give rise to the later practice of the veneration of icons are apostolic. Likewise, the concepts that would give rise to indulgences are also apostolic. For this reason, the Orthodox who criticize indulgences should hold themselves to the same standard with the veneration of icons.

PART 3

LITURGICAL ATTACKS

Both Catholics and Orthodox highly value the sacred liturgy. This is because the liturgy is a way to live out the Christian faith, a means to union with God, and an opportunity to thank God for his many blessings. Catholics and Orthodox also share a common liturgical heritage, as do all of the churches that trace their origins back to the apostles. For these reasons, discussions often arise on the best way to celebrate the liturgy and how the liturgy was celebrated in apostolic times.

Here we'll examine some liturgical objections to the Catholic Church—especially in the Latin rite—that often come up among Orthodox, who claim to have found practices that depart from tradition.

25

"Eucharistic adoration is not a practice established by Jesus"

Some Orthodox object to the practice found in the Latin rite of the Catholic Church called *eucharistic adoration*. This is a devotional practice whereby someone worships Christ in the Eucharist, usually exposed in a monstrance on the altar in a church.

Some Orthodox object to this practice on the grounds that Jesus did not establish it. For instance, Orthodox priest and author Fr. Andrew Stephen Damick states,

> Another distortion of sacramental life comes in the adoration of the Eucharist outside of the context of the act of Communion. . . . The Lord said for us to eat and drink his flesh and blood (John 6:53–56); he said nothing about removing them from that context.[199]

It is true that Jesus did not establish the practice of eucharistic adoration. However, that does not mean that the Church does not have the authority to establish such a practice.

Let's return to a concept we covered in the last objection: the liturgical veneration of icons. There is seemingly no evidence that Jesus or the apostles established this practice. For instance, Orthodox priest and author Fr. John Anthony McGuckin notes the early Church's general aversion to images:

Christianity in the earliest period seems to have shared the aversion common in Judaism (though not an absolute aversion as is demonstrated by the highly decorated second-century synagogue at Dura Europos) to painted representations in religious contexts. The Hellenistic world was so thoroughly immersed in art as a religious medium that both the synagogue and the church turned from it as a part of their apologia against false cult, and Christian thinkers argued instead for the intellectual, spiritual, and moral *mimesis* of God as the only valid depictions of the divine on earth.[200]

Fr. Andrew Louth chimes in by saying the later doctrinal development of icon veneration cannot be found in the fourth-century Fathers.[201] Orthodox priest and author Fr. Laurent A. Cleenewerck echoes this same sentiment: "One will not find in the early Church any clear exposition of the current Eastern Orthodox theology of icons."[202]

In fact, the veneration of icons—as practiced at the time of its dogmatic definition—would have been a perfect practice for the Jews to point to in order to condemn early Christians, if it had existed in such a form in the first century. In the same way that early Christians were accused of being cannibals for their view on the real presence of Christ in the Eucharist, they would certainly have incurred charges of idolatry for this practice. Moreover, some of the early Christians seemed to have held a critical view of the liturgical use of images, since they were still combating pagan idolatry. Yet the concepts that would give rise to the liturgical veneration of icons are certainly apostolic.

What are these concepts, and how does this relate to eucharistic adoration?

Consider the impact the Incarnation had on transforming matter into a vehicle for salvation. The Second Person of the

Trinity became man so that man might be divinized. The *Catechism of the Catholic Church* incorporates Scripture and the Patristic tradition on this subject:

> The Word became flesh to make us *"partakers of the divine nature"*: "For this is why the Word became man, and the Son of God became the Son of Man: so that man, by entering into communion with the Word and thus receiving divine sonship, might become a son of God." "For the Son of God became man so that we might become God." "The only-begotten Son of God, wanting to make us sharers in his divinity, assumed our nature, so that he, made man, might make men gods" (460).

In the Incarnation, the Word took on a human body and a rational soul, which means that the order of creation, at least in some way, participates in the divine life of God. This transformation of the created realm has consequences that reverberate even into liturgical and devotional practices.

Also, the Second Person of the Trinity is a divine person, and this person can actually be seen by those who see his body. This means, in a real sense, that those who looked upon Jesus saw God. It is true that they did not see God's essence, but it is also true that the divine Word is not divided from the humanity he took on, so to look on his humanity is, in a sense, to see the divine.

And so, in a real way, God lifted his prohibition against divine images when he made an image of himself in the Incarnation. This opened up the way for Christians to be able to give, in some sense, an image to God, which was certainly forbidden in the Old Testament. They also reflected on how the veneration given to an image, such as that of a king, finds its end not in the image, but in the thing imaged.

In other words, the veneration given to the image of a king is intended not for the image, but for the king himself.

Additionally, Christians were able to reflect on the distinction between veneration and worship, the former being something that may be due to created beings, whereas the latter is due to God alone.

As Christians further reflected on the doctrinal implications of the Incarnation, the nature of venerating images, and the distinction between veneration and worship, they were able to recognize how venerating icons could be licit. This shows that the Orthodox can accept instances where the Church proposes a post-apostolic practice rooted in apostolic teachings.

A Latin-rite Catholic can use similar argumentation for the practice of eucharistic adoration. Catholics may note that Christ is truly present in the Eucharist. They may also note that the apostles worshiped Jesus. As Latin-rite Catholics reflected on the implications of these truths, along with a consideration of the ancient practice of reserving the Eucharist for distribution to the sick, they realized the liceity of adoring Christ in the Eucharist. After all, if Christ is truly present in the Eucharist, and we have him reserved in our churches, why shouldn't he be given adoration? Simply saying that Jesus didn't establish the practice won't cut it, since the same can be argued against the veneration of icons.

In other words, in the same way that the Church has the authority to introduce the liturgical veneration of icons, based on apostolic concepts, the Church also has the authority to introduce devotion to Christ in the Eucharist, based on apostolic concepts.

Lastly, the Orthodox should consider to what extent their churches have received decree seventeen from the Confession of Dositheus, produced by the Council of Jerusalem in 1672. This was an Orthodox council held in the seventeenth century and led by Patriarch Dositheus of Jerusalem (1641-1707) that produced a confession with a series of decrees and theological propositions and was accepted by the whole of Orthodoxy.

The council states that "The body itself of the Lord and the blood that are in the mystery of the Eucharist ought to be honored in the highest manner, and adored with *latria*."[203]

Latria refers to the worship to be given to God alone. *Dulia*, by contrast, refers to honor, which can be given to creatures. For instance, Christians can honor and respect saints for their heroic and holy lives, but Christians cannot worship the saints, since worship is reserved for God alone.

If this decree has been or should be received within Eastern Orthodoxy, how should Orthodox practically go about adoring the Eucharist with *latria*—that is, worship? Moreover, upon what basis should Latin-rite Catholics refrain from adoring the Eucharist in eucharistic adoration if this decree is true? If it happens to be that this decree is not true, does this mean that the Orthodox have changed their view on what is due to the Eucharist? These are things both Orthodox and Catholics discerning Eastern Orthodoxy should consider.

26

"Catholics changed the order of the sacraments of initiation"

Orthodox often point out that Catholics have changed the order of the sacraments of initiation—from baptism, confirmation, and the Eucharist to baptism, the Eucharist, and confirmation. The Orthodox, on the other hand, have preserved the apostolic tradition of administering all three of these sacraments to an infant all at once. From this, some Orthodox would criticize Catholics as departing from apostolic practices, which the Church allegedly does not have the authority to do. Orthodox then cast doubt on Rome's preservation of the Faith of the first millennium.

Both sides recognize that the Latin rite changed the original order of the sacraments of initiation in the last couple of centuries. This was partly to delay the sacrament of confirmation so that Catholics might receive more catechesis before they received it. This is perfectly within the authority given to the Church when Christ gave St. Peter and the rest of the apostles the power to bind and loose (impose or relax disciplines) and the administration of the keys of the kingdom (Matt. 16:18–19, 18:18). As the "stewards of God's mysteries," the apostles were entrusted with the administration of the sacraments, and this continues through apostolic succession in the episcopate.

The order of the sacraments of initiation should not be a dividing issue between Latin-rite Catholics and the Eastern Orthodox churches. There were churches in the early part of the first millennium that delayed baptism until the candidate was on his deathbed. This was a problematic practice, to say the least, yet Rome did not break communion with the churches that employed it. So too it is in this case.

Additionally, the Orthodox are dealing with their own difficulties concerning the sacraments of initiation—not for infants, but for converts. In some cases, Orthodox will receive a convert by confirmation only, if it can be proven he was validly baptized outside the Orthodox churches. In other cases, such converts are rebaptized, since the Orthodox church receiving the candidate does not recognize the validity of the original baptism. This variance in practice leads some Orthodox to see converts to Orthodoxy who were not received by rebaptism as lesser than those who did get rebaptized—or worse, as non-Orthodox.

It should also be noted that the Orthodox have had to depart from the apostolic practice of having only a bishop administer the sacrament of chrismation—that is, confirmation—because they prioritized keeping the administration of baptism and confirmation together but found it difficult to have a bishop administer these sacraments for every infant. As a solution, the Orthodox adopted the practice of allowing a priest to administer the sacrament of confirmation. So, the Orthodox, too, have made some adjustments in the area of the sacraments of initiation.

Suffice it to say that the Orthodox have their own share of changes and deviations, which should make them a little more understanding toward Latin-rite Catholics.

Lastly, it is worth noting that the Latin rite, in some jurisdictions, has restored the original order of the sacraments of initiation. In 2005, the Diocese of Phoenix in the United States cited the *Catechism*'s declaration that the Eucharist is the "summit" of a Christian's sacramental initiation (1233) to justify its move in this direction.[204] Two years later, Pope Benedict XVI invoked this same concept in his post-synodal apostolic exhortation *Sacramentum Caritatis* (The Sacrament of Charity):

> If the Eucharist is truly the source and summit of the Church's life and mission, it follows that the process of Christian initiation must constantly be directed to the reception of this sacrament. As the synod fathers said, we need to ask ourselves whether in our Christian communities the close link between baptism, confirmation, and Eucharist is sufficiently recognized. It must never be forgotten that our reception of baptism and confirmation is ordered to the Eucharist (17).

Others have heard this call and are working on restoring the sacraments of initiation to their original order. So the Orthodox may be right to point out problems related to altering the order of the sacraments of initiation—and if they are, it turns out that the supreme organ of the Magisterium is addressing the issue, as it is well within the Church's competence to do.

27

"Catholics changed the apostolic administration of baptism"

Some Orthodox criticize Catholics on the grounds that the Church changed the apostolic administration of baptism—that is, from *immersion* to *affusion* (or pouring). The Orthodox tend to argue that the apostolic practice was by immersion, so they claim that Latin-rite Catholics have deviated from the apostolic practice.

It is not necessarily true that baptism was always done by immersion in apostolic times. For instance, it is not certain that the 3,000 baptized on the Day of Pentecost in Acts 2:41 were initiated by full immersion, as it is possible that there wasn't enough water available to do this. However, a Latin-rite Catholic can admit that immersion is the ideal, as the Catholic theologian Lawrence Feingold says:

> The matter for baptism is the washing with water, which can be done by immersion or by pouring, although immersion provides a more adequate representation.[205]

Some Orthodox may not be content with this, as they may argue that the ideal should always be upheld, especially since immersion best signifies the image of death and resurrection, which Romans 6:1–4 tells us baptism signifies. It is true that

St. Paul describes baptism this way, but we also have Acts 2:17 and Acts 10:44–45, which describe the Holy Spirit as being poured out. Though the context for the imagery in these verses is not baptism, it does describe the action of the Holy Spirit, who is given in baptism.

Additionally, we have the *Didache*, a Christian catechism written either in the first or second century, which attests to the validity of baptism by pouring:

> But if thou hast not living water, then baptize in other water; and if thou art not able in cold, then in warm. But if though has neither, then pour water on the head thrice in the name of the Father and of the Son and of the Holy Spirit.[206]

It is true that the *Didache* sees immersion as the ordinary way to baptize, with affusion being a backup alternative, but it at least testifies to the validity of affusion in the early Church. Thus, the difference between Latin-rite Catholics and the Orthodox churches is not one of validity, but of practice. Considering that Latin-rite Catholics can acknowledge the practice of immersion as the ideal, and the matter is not one of validity, this should not be a dividing issue.

Yet this does raise a question. Does the Church have the authority to alter some aspects of the apostolic administration of the sacraments? Both Catholics and Orthodox must answer in the affirmative, since both the Catholic Church and the Orthodox churches have done so. In the case of the Orthodox, they have made some modifications to the minister of the sacrament of chrismation (confirmation). In the Apostolic Era, confirmation was administered by the apostles and their successors, the bishops.[207] As the Church grew, it became increasingly hard for the bishop to baptize and confirm every child, so the East tended to delegate the power to confirm to a priest in order keep the sacraments of baptism and confirmation together, whereas the West preserved the earlier custom of having the bishop administer confirmation,[208] albeit with the consequence of separating it from baptism.

Thus, both the East and the West have deviated from the apostolic practice concerning the sacraments of initiation in one way or another. This means that neither Latin-rite Catholics nor Eastern Orthodox should see practical alterations to some apostolic practices as a dividing issue.

28

"Catholics venerate some Orthodox saints but claim that Orthodox are schismatics"

It has become quite popular for Orthodox to point out that some of the Eastern Catholic churches liturgically commemorate a few Orthodox saints, including Gregory Palamas (1296-1359). They will bring this up and then note that Catholicism sees Eastern Orthodoxy as schismatic. The takeaway seems to be that Catholicism is internally incoherent, since it venerates schismatic saints.

In order to alleviate the tension, it would first be helpful to note what schism is. *Schism* is defined by canon law and the *Catechism* as "the refusal of submission to the Roman pontiff or of communion with the members of the Church subject to him" (CCC 2089).

Do the Orthodox churches refuse to submit to the pope's authority? Yes—which means, objectively speaking, that they are in a state of schism. It is true that they have valid local churches and valid sacraments (see the Second Vatican Council's decree *Unitatis Redintegratio, On Ecumenism,* 14–15), and it is true that 1965 saw the lifting of the 1054 anathemas between Patriarch Michael Cerularius and Cardinal Humbertus. But the lifting of those anathemas was for specific people in 1054, which says nothing about Orthodox today.

It is certainly possible for a valid local church to be in schism. It is also possible for someone who has not been formally declared excommunicated still to be in schism. Thus, neither of these points takes away from the force of the canonical definition of schism.

Although all of this is true, it is also possible for someone who is, objectively speaking, in a state of schism to be unaware of this or not to be fully culpable for this state. For instance, it may be supposed that the majority of Eastern Orthodox are not aware that they are in a state of schism. Even if they have heard Catholics say this sort of thing, that does not mean they know that it is accurate in God's eyes. For this reason, a level of ignorance, which reduces culpability (see CCC 1735 and 1793), may remain.

There is historical precedent for this in the case of Spanish conquistadors and Native Americans. Francisco de Vitoria, O.P., a Dominican theologian in the sixteenth century, said the following about the culpability of Native Americans who rejected the gospel proclamation of the conquistadors:

> The Indians in question are not bound, directly the Christian faith is announced to them, to believe it, in such a way that they commit mortal sin by not believing it, merely because it has been declared and announced to them that Christianity is the true religion and that Christ is the Savior and Redeemer of the world, without miracle or any other proof or persuasion. . . . For if before hearing anything of the Christian religion they were excused, they are put under no fresh obligation by a simple declaration and announcement of this kind, for such announcement is no proof or incentive to belief.[209]

This means that simply hearing the gospel proclamation without being given good reasons to believe it does not necessarily impute culpability or dispel ignorance. De Vitoria goes on to say,

> It is not sufficiently clear to me that the Christian faith has yet been so put before the aborigines and announced to them that they are bound to believe it or commit fresh sin. I say this because . . . they are not bound to believe unless the Faith be put before them with persuasive demonstration. Now, I hear of no miracles or signs or religious patterns of life; nay, on the contrary, I hear of many scandals and cruel crimes and acts of impiety. Hence, it does not appear that the Christian religion has been preached to them with such sufficient propriety and piety that they are bound to acquiesce in it, even though many religious and other ecclesiastics seem both by their lives and example and their diligent preaching to have bestowed sufficient pains and industry in this business, had they not been hindered therein by men who were intent on other things.

Essentially, de Vitoria argues that the proclamation of the gospel is hindered by scandalous behavior on the part of Christians. Because of this, there is reduced culpability—and certainly insufficient culpability to establish mortal sin—for those who do not find the message persuasive. At the very least, this shows in Catholic tradition that there is a concept of a reduction of culpability for those who have heard the gospel in a less than convincing way.

We may now make some applications to the Orthodox. Has the average Orthodox heard persuasive reasons for why the Catholic Church has the fullness of the Faith and why Catholics claim that the Church Christ established fully "subsists in the Catholic Church" (*Lumen Gentium* 8)? Has he been given persuasive reasons to believe the claims about papal primacy and papal infallibility as expressed at the First Vatican Council? Has the average Orthodox truly been presented these things in a convincing manner? A simple conversation with the average Orthodox will answer this question, as it is painfully clear that most Orthodox tend to have a straw man in mind when they consider Catholicism or the papacy.

It is important to consider how someone who is not a formal member of the Catholic Church could be nonetheless united to the Church, outside which there is no salvation. The 1949 Letter of the Sacred Congregation of the Holy Office to Archbishop Richard J. Cushing notes:

> It must not be thought that any kind of desire of entering the Church suffices that one may be saved. It is necessary that the desire by which one is related to the Church be animated by perfect charity.[210]

This means that it is possible to be united to the Church, outside which there is no salvation, through the virtue of charity, even though saving grace is ordinarily given in the sacraments. The Orthodox have valid sacraments, so it is at least possible that they have access to the "perfect charity," mentioned in the Holy Office's letter, required for implicit membership in the one true Church.

The letter also notes,

> This desire need not always be explicit, as it is in catechumens; but when a person is involved in invincible ignorance God accepts also an implicit desire, so called because it is included in that good disposition of soul

whereby a person wishes his will to be conformed to the will of God.

In other words, as long as an Orthodox has an implicit desire to enter the Catholic Church and would have joined it if he had known that it is the fullness of the Church Christ established, then it is possible that God accepts his disposition. Thus, if a person is invincibly ignorant about the claims of the Catholic Church, has an implicit desire to enter it, and possesses perfect charity, it is possible that he is in fact a living member of the one Church, outside which there is no salvation, albeit invisibly and even unknowingly.

It is certainly difficult to identify with any kind of certitude whether a specific person meets these criteria, which is why it is important to call all people to formally join the Catholic Church. Moreover, it is highly debatable how common mitigating circumstances such as invincible ignorance are, given the widespread availability of truth in the world today. Certainly, some may argue on the basis of Pope Benedict XVI's encyclical letter *Spe Salvi* that the majority of humans are open to God (see 46).

The Second Vatican Council, however, seems to take the view that people, more often than not, have exchanged truth for a lie (*Lumen Gentium* 16). This gives the impression that the council fathers did not think that mitigating circumstances are very common. Consequently, there is an immediate danger for anyone who is a non-Catholic, and it is absolutely imperative that such people be presented with the truth of the Catholic Church and embrace it.

Having considered these things, we may turn our attention to Orthodox saints such as Gregory Palamas. Is it possible that he was not presented the truth about the Catholic Church in a convincing way and was animated by perfect charity while maintaining an implicit desire to enter Christ's Church? Not only is it possible, but we can have moral certitude that this was the case, since Rome approved of his liturgical veneration in 1974, by publishing a liturgical book that includes his feast day.[211] Given the above, there isn't an internal inconsistency in the Catholic Church's claims about schism and the veneration of some saints who were not formally in union with the Church but were united with it informally.

Lastly, it is worthwhile to anticipate an objection that Orthodox may raise at this point. Some may say that with the Catholics acceptance of the canonization of Gregory Palamas—Catholics will canonize anyone! However, this does not follow, since the Catholic Church maintains the distinction between those who start a schism and those who are born into a schism. The former will never be canonized. There is also a difference between someone who was never a formal Catholic vs. someone who was a formal Catholic and left the Catholic Church for a schismatic communion. The latter will never be canonized. In other words, while the Church is willing to grant significant leeway in who may be deemed to have lived within God's grace, the Church recognizes some standards in the canonization process that may never be transgressed.

29

"Catholics have clown Masses"

One of the least reasonable, but highly emotional, objections a Catholic may encounter when considering Orthodoxy is the claim that Catholicism is not the Church established by Christ because it has clown Masses.

This is actually an argument employed by some popular Orthodox apologists, and their followers, in online forums. In fact, when one Orthodox apologist was cornered in a debate with a Catholic apologist, he changed the topic of the discussion and cried out, "You guys have clown Masses!" That was the extent of his argument—and it was highly effective, considering that many people make decisions based on their emotions more than their intellect. Sadly, this poorly-thought-out and inconsistent objection carries a significant amount of rhetorical force.

Before addressing the argument directly, I want to firmly state that I sympathize with anyone who has ever experienced liturgical abuse. The liturgy should be an occasion of growing in sanctity, but sadly, liturgical abuse often removes a person from a prayerful experience and places him in a frustrated state. Such things not only have the potential to scandalize us, but also impede our progress in holiness, since they can understandably cause us to become preoccupied with what we have experienced instead of prayerfully participating in the Church's liturgy. Consequently, liturgical abuse should not be tolerated, and pious Catholics who have experienced liturgical abuse should be accompanied by their pastors and given the proper means to find healing. As one who has experienced liturgical abuses and has earned war wounds for speaking out against them, I can personally testify that this is an area where many pastors are underserving their flock.

As to the Orthodox who think "you guys have clown Masses" is a slam dunk against Catholicism, why is this argument poorly thought out? Because clown Masses are liturgical *abuses*, not what the Catholic Church calls for in its liturgical rubrics and instructions on the sacred liturgy. For this reason, clown Masses, and other such abuses, cannot be considered reflective of what the Catholic Church has promulgated.

Literal clown Masses—which, it is a shame to concede, have occurred—are so rare that they can hardly be said to represent the Catholic Church's liturgical life. That being said, there may be other liturgical abuses that are more common, and the Magisterium and the popes, up to and including Pope Francis,[212] have condemned them.

Does such an admission disprove the Catholic claim that it is the church that Christ established? Certainly not. Consider the fact that there are many instances of serious liturgical abuse in the Old Testament, and yet these did not invalidate the Israelite's claim to being the covenant community of God. We simply have to look at instances such as 1 Samuel 2:21–36, where the high priest's sons, Hophni and Phinehas, engaged in deplorable acts related to God's worship. Additionally, we can consider the offensive liturgical sacrifices the people brought to God in the days of the prophet Malachi, thus earning a scathing rebuke from God in the first chapter of the biblical book named for that prophet.

Despite such offensive acts, these liturgical abuses did not disprove Israel's covenant claims. Since Orthodox affirm the truthfulness of this point in their acceptance of the Old Testament, they should not use this inconsistent and hypocritical argument against Catholics.

Why "hypocritical"? The "clown Masses" objection claims that Christ did not establish the Catholic Church because there are some in the Church who abuse the liturgy. However, there are plenty of cases where Orthodox individuals abuse good things, too. For instance, a prominent bishop recently baptized the infants of an open and unrepentant same-sex couple. Given that there was little hope that the children would be raised in the Orthodox faith, many Orthodox were scandalized by this liturgical event, which the same-sex couple paraded on social media. Yet Orthodox would not argue that the Greek Orthodox Church ceases to be one of the churches established by Christ because some of its bishops have abused the administration of the sacraments. Thus, Orthodox should avoid employing this argument against Catholics if they wish to be fair and consistent.

Lastly, I would argue that serious liturgical abuses are not as common as some Orthodox, and even some Catholics, may claim. In some cases, the claims are exaggerated or stem from an overly scrupulous understanding of the liturgy. In other cases, the critic may be ignorant of liturgical history and rubrics. That being said, there are instances of serious liturgical abuse—as I have personally witnessed and spoken against at a great cost—and these should be immediately fixed by the shepherds of the Church lest they allow their flock to become scandalized.

30

"Catholics use unleavened bread for the Eucharist"

One of the most peculiar objections a Catholic may encounter from Eastern Orthodoxy is that Catholics use unleavened bread (*azymes*) for the Eucharist.

It must be said at the outset that this refers mostly to the Latin rite. Most Eastern (or Byzantine) Catholics use leavened bread, as the Orthodox do.

According to the Orthodox, those Catholics who use unleavened bread are guilty of *Judaizing*—that is, following Old Testament Jewish rites, or "eating at the table of the Jews"[213]—instead of following the New Covenant practice. Some have even gone so far as to say the Catholic Eucharist is invalid because of this.[214]

As odd as this charge may sound, the issue behind it was a major problem between East and West, historically speaking. In fact, Patriarch John of Antioch in the eleventh century said that the question of leavened and unleavened bread for the Eucharist is the main cause of the schism between the East and the West![215] That's right—not the papacy, nor the *filioque*, but *azymes*!

Catholics should admit that there is fourth-century evidence that the Western Church had a custom of using leavened bread, and there aren't any references to using unleavened bread in the West until the end of the eighth century.[216] Yet there are some advantages to using unleavened bread. It is less likely to spoil as quickly as leavened bread and less likely to break into crumbs that may fall on the floor and be treated in a profane way.

What's more, there is a biblical argument for the use of unleavened bread, since leaven sometimes refers to sin and hypocrisy, as in the case of Matthew 16:6. Additionally, in the context of the Easter liturgy, St. Paul says,

> Your boasting is not good. Do you not know that a little leaven leavens the whole lump? Cleanse out the old leaven that you may be a new lump, as you really are unleavened. For Christ, our paschal lamb, has been sacrificed. Let us, therefore, celebrate the festival, not with the old leaven, the leaven of malice and evil, but with the unleavened bread of sincerity and truth (1 Cor. 5:6–8).

Note how Paul equates leaven with sin and urges the churches to celebrate the feast with unleavened bread, which is a symbol for truth.

On the other hand, some may argue that Jesus used leavened bread at the Last Supper, since the Greek word used in Matthew 26:26 was not *azumos* (unleavened), but *artos*, which may refer to a loaf of bread.[217] However, this is unlikely, as the context of the meal in verse 17 is the feast of unleavened bread, also known as the Passover meal.* In verse 17, the term *azumos* is used, and Jesus, as an observant Jew, would have certainly used unleavened bread to celebrate the Passover. Moreover, the term *artos* can refer to leavened or unleavened bread. For one example, the shewbread used in

---

* Some have disputed whether the Last Supper was a Passover meal. For a good response to this objection, see Brant Pitre, *Jesus and the Last Supper.*

the Old Testament was unleavened and the Septuagint (the Greek version of the Old Testament) in Exodus 25:30 uses the term *artos* to describe it.[218]

In other words, there are good arguments for using either form of bread. Both customs are permitted in the Catholic Church, and the use of unleavened bread for the Eucharist should not stand in the way of Catholic and Orthodox reunion.

Conclusion

There are many reasons why some Catholics are discerning Eastern Orthodoxy. As they begin this process of discernment, they inevitably encounter some arguments that may be new to them, especially considering that common objections to Catholicism usually come from Protestantism. So, this initial lack of unfamiliarity may jolt their faith as they hear arguments they've likely never considered before. This may cause them to develop some skepticism toward their faith, which possibly reinforces some existing concerns they already had.

In many cases, the lack of Catholic engagement with Orthodox apologetics in popular circles leads some to think there aren't any adequate responses to Orthodox objections. They may even conclude that their initial reasons for being a Catholic were poorly founded, especially if these reasons were based on the papacy and they are not able to find solutions to the anti-papal apologetics they encounter in some Orthodox circles. In some cases, these Catholics convert to Orthodoxy without having heard sufficient argumentation in response to the Orthodox apologetics that convinced them to leave communion with Rome.

In this work, I have attempted to respond to some of the most common objections discerning Catholics will encounter when exposed to Orthodox apologetics. It is my hope that those who have not yet left the Catholic Church will see that there are sufficient responses to Orthodox objections to Catholicism. I have also attempted to show that the historical roots of Orthodoxy are shot through with Catholicism, so that if the Catholic claims to the papacy or the *filioque* are untrue, then that is a pox on both the houses, Catholics *and* Orthodox. I also hope that this work will have shown Catholic converts to Orthodoxy that they may not have left Catholicism for the right reasons, and if they truly want to be orthodox, they must embrace the Catholic roots of Orthodoxy.

Though the intended audience of this work is primarily Catholics discerning Orthodoxy, I also hope that this work will benefit Protestant converts to Orthodoxy and even cradle Orthodox. This work should have demonstrated that union with Catholicism is not an abandonment of Orthodoxy, but a full embrace of Orthodoxy's history and tradition that Orthodoxy itself cannot provide.

Lastly, it must be admitted that there are numerous objections to raise against Catholicism that this book doesn't cover, plus objections to my answers in this work. However, I hope to have at least demonstrated that common Orthodox objections to Catholicism are not the slam dunk some seem to think they are, and in many cases, the arguments made by the Orthodox can be turned back around on them. Thus, to employ such argumentation against Catholicism is to engage in the use of unequal weights (Prov. 20:10)—and that is something condemned in the same Sacred Scripture both Catholics and Orthodox revere.

A Summary of the First Seven Ecumenical Councils

Nicaea I (325): This council is the first ecumenical council and specifically combated the heresy of Arianism, which denied the divinity of Jesus. The council infallibly taught that Jesus is of the same substance as God the Father, expressing belief in his full divinity.

Constantinople I (381): This was a local council that was later accepted as the second ecumenical council. It emphasized the divinity of the Holy Spirit against those who denied his full divinity.

Ephesus I (431): This council especially dealt with the question of whether Jesus is two persons (Nestorianism) or one. It infallibly taught that Jesus is one person and Mary is the Mother of God (meaning that the one she gave birth to is fully divine).

Chalcedon (451): This council addressed those who claimed that Jesus has only one nature. It infallibly taught that though Jesus is one person, he has two natures: human and divine. These two natures are not separate or mixed, but they are distinct.

Constantinople II (553): This council was assembled due to the confusion some had over the Council of Chalcedon, which was seen by some as teaching Nestorianism. The council was called to show that this was not the case and to deal with the writings of Theodore of Mopsuestia, Theodoret of Cyrrhus, and Ibas of Edessa. It condemned their writings and emphasized its condemnation of Nestorianism.

Constantinople III (680–681): The sixth ecumenical council addressed the question of whether Jesus had two wills (Dyothelitism) or only one will (Monothelitism). The council infallibly taught that because Jesus has two natures, he also has two wills.

Nicaea II (787): This council addressed the question of iconography in the Church. It distinguished between the honor that is given to the saints and worship that is due to God. It also determined that the veneration of icons is permitted and is not the sin of idolatry.

About the Author

Michael Lofton is an Eastern Catholic and a graduate of Christendom College Graduate School of Theology, where he received his master of arts in theological studies (*cum laude*) in 2018. He is currently working on a doctorate in theology with Pontifex University and is writing a dissertation on the Magisterium of the Catholic Church. Michael has interviewed many leading figures in contemporary theology as the founder and host of *Reason & Theology* and is the founder of the Maximus Institute, where he teaches on various theological subjects.

Endnotes

1   L. Duchesne, *Autonomies Ecclésiastiques: Eglises Séparées,* (Paris: Fontemoing 1905), 164–65, as quoted in Alexander Schmemann, *The Historical Road of Eastern Orthodoxy* (Crestwood, NY: St. Vladimir's Seminary Press, 1977), 241.

2   Francis Dvornik, *Byzantium and the Roman Primacy* (New York: Fordham University Press, 1966), 157.

3   Michael Azkoul, *The Teachings of the Holy Orthodox Church*, vol. 1 (Buena Vista, CO: Dormition Skete, 1986), 221.

4   John Meyendorff, *Orthodoxy and Catholicity* (New York, NY: Sheed & Ward, 1966), 19.

5   Gregory the Great, *Registrum Epistolarum*, 5.18, in *Nicene and Post-Nicene Fathers: A Select Library of the Christian Church*, ed. Philip Schaff and Henry Wace, vol. 12 (Peabody, MA: Hendrickson 2004), 167.

6   Michael Pomazansky and Seraphim Rose, *Orthodox Dogmatic Theology: A Concise Exposition* (Platina, CA: Saint Herman of Alaska Brotherhood, 1997), 228.

7   See the first session in Richard Price and Michael Gaddis, *The Acts of the Council of Chalcedon*, vol. 1 (Liverpool: Liverpool University Press, 2005), 129.

8   Richard Price and Phil Booth, *The Acts of the Lateran Synod of 649* (Liverpool: Liverpool Univ. Press, 2016), 143–44.

9   Price and Booth, *The Acts of the Lateran Synod of 649*, 143 as quoted in A. Edward Siecienski, *The Papacy and the Orthodox: Sources and History of a Debate* (New York: Oxford University Press, 2017), 200.

10 Richard Price, *The Acts of the Second Council of Nicaea (787)* (Liverpool: Liverpool University Press, 2020), 180.

11 Justinian calls Rome the "caput omnium ecclesiarum." See *Codex Justinianus*, 1, 1, as quoted in Dvornik, *Byzantium and the Roman Primacy*, 73.

12 Price, *The Acts of the Second Council of Nicaea (787)*, 182.

13 Laurent Cleenewerck, *His Broken Body: Understanding and Healing the Schism Between the Roman Catholic and Eastern Orthodox Churches* (Washington, DC: Euclid University Consortiuim Press, 2013), 214.

14 John Panteleimon Manoussakis, *For the Unity of All: Contributions to the Theological Dialogue Between East and West* (Eugene, OR: Cascade Books, 2015), 31.

15 Ibid., 25.

16 Alexander Schmemann, "The Idea of Primacy in Orthodox Eccesiology," in John Meyendorff, *The Primacy of Peter: Essays in Ecclesiology and the Early Church* (Crestwood, NY: St. Vladimir's Seminary Press, 1992), 151.

17 Andrew S. Damick, *Orthodoxy and Heterodoxy: Finding the Way to Christ in a Complicated Religious Landscape* (Chesterton, IN: Ancient Faith, 2017), 68.

18 Meyendorff, *Orthodoxy and Catholicity*, 141.

19 Richard Price and Thomas Graumann, *The Council of Ephesus of 431: Documents and Proceedings* (Liverpool: Liverpool University Press, 2022), 131.

20 Richard Price, *The Acts of the Council of Constantinople of 553: With Related Texts on the Three Chapters Controversy*, vol. 1 (Liverpool: Liverpool University Press, 2012), 56.

21 Leo the Great, Letter 33, in *Nicene and Post-Nicene Fathers: A Select Library of the Christian Church*, vol. 12, 47.

22 Lawrence Jerome King, "The Authoritative Weight of Non-Definitive Magisterial Teaching" (Ph.D. diss., The Catholic University of America 2016), 208, https://cuislandora.wrlc.org/islandora/object/cuislandora%3A40891/datastream/PDF/view.

23 See Siecienski, *The Papacy and the Orthodox: Sources and History of a Debate*, 205.

24 This claim by the Orthodox may be seen in John H. Erickson, *The Challenge of Our Past: Studies in Orthodox Canon Law and Church History* (Crestwood, NY: St. Vladimir's Seminary Press, 1991), 79.

25 *De primatu papae*, PG 149, 708B, as quoted in Dvornik, *Byzantium and the Roman Primacy*, 161.

26 Dvornik, *Byzantium and the Roman Primacy*, 161.

27 See *Epistle 26,* in *Ante-Nicene Fathers: The Writings of the Fathers Down to A.D. 325*, ed. Alexander Roberts, James Donaldson, and A. Cleveland Coxe, vol. 5 (Peabody, MA: Hendrickson, 2004), 305.

28 Extracts from the Acts in, *Nicene and Post-Nicene Fathers: A Select Library of the Christian Church*, ed. Philip Schaff and Henry Wace, vol. 14 (Peabody, MA: Hendrickson, 2004), 222.

29 Ibid.

30 Ibid., 223.

31 Schmemann, *The Historical Road of Eastern Orthodoxy*, 241.

32 See § 5, xv, in Internet Modern History Sourcebook: "Encyclical of the Eastern Patriarchs, 1848: A Reply to the Epistle of Pope Pius IX, 'to the Easterns,'" Internet History Sourcebooks, November 1998, https://sourcebooks.fordham.edu/mod/1848orthodoxencyclical.asp.

33 See § 6 in Internet Modern History Sourcebook: "Encyclical of the Eastern Patriarchs, 1848: A Reply to the Epistle of Pope Pius IX, 'to the Easterns.'"

34 A. Edward Siecienski, *The Filioque: History of a Doctrinal Controversy* (New York, NY: Oxford Univ. Press, 2010), 10.

35 Ibid., 9.

36 Timothy Ware, *The Orthodox Church* (London, England: Penguin Books, 1997), 211, 217.

37 *On the Trinity*, 5, 14:15, in *Nicene and Post-Nicene Fathers: A Select Library of the Christian Church*, ed. Philip Schaff and Henry Wace, vol. 3 (Peabody, MA: Hendrickson, 2004), 95.

38 Siecienski, *The Filioque: History of a Doctrinal Controversy*, 65.

39 Ware, *The Orthodox Church*, 217.

40 Maximus the Confessor, *Quaestiones et dubia*, 34, ed. José Declerk, CCG 10 (Turnhout, Belgium: Brepols, 1982), 151, as quoted in Siecienski, *The Filioque: History of a Doctrinal Controversy*, 77.

41 Maximus the Confessor, *Opsculum* 10 (PG 91, 136), as quoted in Siecienski, *The Filioque: History of a Doctrinal Controversy*, 80–81.

42 Ware, *The Orthodox Church*, 212.

43 Andrew Louth, "Is Development of Doctrine a Valid Category for Orthodox Theology?," in *Orthodoxy and Western Culture: A Collection of Essays Honoring Jaroslav Pelikan on His Eightieth Birthday*, ed. Patrick Henry and Valerie Hotchkiss (Crestwood, NY: St. Vladimir's Seminary Press, 2005), 47.

44 See Siecienski, *The Filioque: History of a Doctrinal Controversy*, 77.

45 Damick, *Orthodoxy and Heterodoxy: Finding the Way to Christ in a Complicated Religious Landscape*, 69.

46 Erick Ybarra, *The Filioque: Revisiting the Doctrinal Debate Between Catholics and Orthodox*, 2nd ed. (Florida: Classical Christian Thought, 2022), 9.

47 Ware, *The Orthodox Church*, 213.

48 Siecienski, *The Filioque: History of a Doctrinal Controversy*, 10.

49 Manoussakis, *For the Unity of All: Contributions to the Theological Dialogue Between East and West*, 17–18.

50 Damick, *Orthodoxy and Heterodoxy: Finding the Way to Christ in a Complicated Religious Landscape*, 69.

51 Clark Carlton, *The Truth: What Every Roman Catholic Should Know About the Orthodox Church* (Salisbury, MA: Regina Orthodox Press, 1999), 101.

52 Joseph Gill, *The Council of Florence* (New York: Cambridge University Press, 2011), 121.

53 Norman P. Tanner, *Decrees of the Ecumenical Councils, Volume 1: Nicaea I–Lateran V* (London: Sheed & Ward, 1990), 230.

54 See St. Gregory the Great, *Dial.* 4, 39: PL 77, 396, as quoted in § 1031 in *Catechism of the Catholic Church: With Modifications from the Editio Typica* (New York, NY: Doubleday, 2003).

55 Ludwig Ott, *Fundamentals of Catholic Dogma*, ed. James Bastible (Rockford, IL: Tan Books and Publishers, 1974), 485.

56 Ware, *The Orthodox Church*, 255.

57 Cleenewerck, *His Broken Body: Understanding and Healing the Schism Between the Roman Catholic and Eastern Orthodox Churches*, 359.

58 Ware, *The Orthodox Church*, 255.

59 Ibid., 203.

60 Philip Schaff and David S. Schaff, *The Creeds of Christendom: With A History and Critical Notes*, 6th ed., vol. 1 (Grand Rapids, MI: Baker Books, 2007), 65–66.

61 Damick, *Orthodoxy and Heterodoxy: Finding the Way to Christ in a Complicated Religious Landscape*, 89.

62 Dumitru Stăniloae, *The Experience of God: Orthodox Dogmatic Theology*, vol. 6 (Brookline, MA: Holy Cross Orthodox Press, 2013), 94.

63 J. Hontheim, "Hell," in *The Catholic Encyclopedia*, vol. 7 (New York: Robert Appleton, 1910; online ed. New Advent), https://www.newadvent.org/cathen/07207a.htm.

64 Ware, *The Orthodox Church*, 224.

65 Norman P. Tanner, *Decrees of the Ecumenical Councils, Volume 2: Trent to Vatican II* (London: Sheed & Ward, 1990), 667.

66 Charlton T. Lewis and Charles Short, "Reatus," in *Harpers' Latin Dictionary: A New Latin Dictionary* (Oxford, NY: Harper & Brothers, 1891), 1529.

67 Damick, *Orthodoxy and Heterodoxy: Finding the Way to Christ in a Complicated Religious Landscape*, 80.

68 Dennis Bratcher, ed., "The Confession of Dositheus (Eastern Orthodox, 1672)," The Voice, Dennis Bratcher, 2018, accessed October 12, 2022,

http://www.crivoice.org/creeddositheus.html, decree sixteen.

69   See canon 121 of Carthage, in Agapios and Nicodemus, *The Rudder*, trans.
     D. Cummings (Chicago, IL: Orthodox Christian Educational Society,
     1957), 688. Cf. Denzinger 223, in Peter Hünermann et al., *Compendium
     of Creeds, Definitions, and Declarations on Matters of Faith and Morals* (San
     Francisco: Ignatius Press, 2012), 82.

70   Denzinger 267, in Hünermann et al., *Compendium of Creeds, Definitions, and
     Declarations on Matters of Faith and Morals*, 99.

71   Damick, *Orthodoxy and Heterodoxy: Finding the Way to Christ in a Complicated
     Religious Landscape*, 82.

72   Ott, *Fundamentals of Catholic Dogma*, 202.

73   F. Holweck, "Immaculate Conception," in *The Catholic Encyclopedia*, vol. 7,
     accessed September 23, 2022, https://www.newadvent.org/cathen/07674d.htm.

74   Carlton, *The Truth: What Every Roman Catholic Should Know About the
     Orthodox Church*, 159.

75   Ibid., 159.

76   Damick, *Orthodoxy and Heterodoxy: Finding the Way to Christ in a Complicated
     Religious Landscape*, 81.

77   Christiaan W. Kappes, *The Immaculate Conception: Why Thomas Aquinas
     Denied, While John Duns Scotus, Gregory Palamas, and Mark Eugenicus
     Professed the Absolute Immaculate Existence of Mary* (New Bedford, MA:
     Academy of the Immaculate, 2014), 164.

78   Manoussakis, *For the Unity of All: Contributions to the Theological Dialogue
     Between East and West*, 5.

79   Carlton, *The Truth: What Every Roman Catholic Should Know About the
     Orthodox Church*, 89.

80   Ott, *Fundamentals of Catholic Dogma*, 220.

81   Damick, *Orthodoxy and Heterodoxy: Finding the Way to Christ in a Complicated
     Religious Landscape*, 75.

82   Ibid., 74.

83   Lattier, "The Orthodox Rejection of Doctrinal Development," *Pro Ecclesia:
     A Journal of Catholic and Evangelical Theology* 20, no. 4 (2011): 390, https://
     doi.org/10.1177/106385121102000408.

84   Peter M. J. Stravinskas, ed., *Our Sunday Visitor's Catholic Encyclopedia*
     (Huntington, IN: Our Sunday Visitor, 1991), 303.

85   Vincent of Lérins, *A Commonitory*, chap. 23 in *Nicene and Post-Nicene*

Fathers: A Select Library of the Christian Church, ed. Philip Schaff and Henry Wace, vol. 11 (Peabody, MA: Hendrickson, 2004), 147–48.

86 Lattier, "The Orthodox Rejection of Doctrinal Development," 409.

87 Extracts from the Acts, in *Nicene and Post-Nicene Fathers: A Select Library of the Christian Church*, vol. 14, 534.

88 Andrew Louth, "Is Development of Doctrine a Valid Category for Orthodox Theology?," 47.

89 Ware, *The Orthodox Church*, 289.

90 Ibid.

91 Isabel Florence Hapgood, *Service Book of the Holy Orthodox-Catholic Apostolic Church* (Englewood, NJ: Antiochian Orthodox Christian Archdiocese of North America, 1996), 290.

92 "The Mystery of Penance," Metropolitan Cantor Institute, Byzantine Catholic Archeparchy of Pittsburgh, accessed August 3, 2022, https://mci.archpitt.org/liturgy/Penance.html.

93 Tanner, *Decrees of the Ecumenical Councils, Volume 2: Trent to Vatican II*, 816.

94 Joseph Cullen Ayer, *A Source Book for Ancient Church History: From the Apostolic Age to the Close of the Conciliar Period* (New York: Scribner, 1941), 536.

95 Erick Ybarra, *The Papacy: Revisiting the Debate between Catholics and Orthodox* (Steubenville, OH: Emmaus Road Press, 2022), 406–7.

96 Robert B. Eno, *The Rise of the Papacy* (Eugene, OR: Wipf & Stock, 2008), 131.

97 Henry Chadwick, *East and West: The Making of a Rift in the Church: From Apostolic Times until the Council of Florence* (Oxford, NY: Oxford University Press, 2003), 46.

98 Schmemann, *The Historical Road of Eastern Orthodoxy*, 241.

99 Siecienski, *The Papacy and the Orthodox: Sources and History of a Debate*, 185.

100 PL 63, 444A; *Col. Avel. Epist.* 159, CSEL, vol. 35, 608, 2; as quoted in Dvornik, *Byzantium and the Roman Primacy*, 61.

101 See Dvornik, *Byzantium and the Roman Primacy*, 61, and Eno, *The Rise of the Papacy*,131.

102 Peter Batiffol, *Catholicism and Papacy: Some Anglican and Russian Difficulties*, trans. Oliver Rodie Vassal-Phillips (London: Sands, 1925), 123.

103 The Letter of Pope Agatho, in *Nicene and Post-Nicene Fathers: A Select Library of the Christian Church*, vol. 14, 331–32

104 Ibid., 349.

105 Maximus the Confessor, *Opuscula theologica et polemica*, 11, PG 91, 137–140;
     English translation in Adam G. Cooper, *The Body in St. Maximus the
     Confessor: Holy Flesh, Wholly Deified* (Oxford: Oxford University Press,
     2005), 181 as quoted in Siecienski, *The Papacy and the Orthodox: Sources and
     History of a Debate*, 201–2.

106 Quoted in George C. Berthold, *Maximus Confessor: Selected Writings*
     (Mahwah, NJ: Paulist Press, 1985), 23.

107 For more on the Christological implications involved in this debate, see
     Joseph P. Farrell, *Disputations with Pyrrhus* (Waymart, PA: St. Tikhon's
     Monastery Press, 2014).

108 Denzinger 251, in Heinrich Denzinger, *The Sources of Catholic Dogma*, trans.
     Roy J. Deferrari (Fitzwilliam, NH: Loreto Publications, 2010), 99.

109 See T.3, B. 2, C.2, A.2, TH. 14, N.654, in Joachim Salaverri and Michaele
     Nicolau, *On the Church of Christ: On Holy Scripture*, trans. Kenneth Baker
     (Ramsey, NJ: Keep the Faith, 2015), 239.

110 Pauline Allen and Bronwen Neil, *Conflict and Negotiation in the Early
     Church: Letters from Late Antiquity, Translated from the Greek, Latin, and Syriac*
     (Washington, D.C.: The Catholic University of America Press, 2020), 184.

111 Farrell, *Disputations with Pyrrhus*, 49.

112 Dvornik, *Byzantium and the Roman Primacy*, 92.

113 See Bronwen Neil, *Seventh-Century Popes and Martyrs: The Political Hagiography
     of Anastasius Bibliothecarius* (Turnhout: Brepols, 2006), 155.

114 Salaverri and Nicolau, *On the Church of Christ: On Holy Scripture*, 239.

115 John Chapman, *The Condemnation of Pope Honorius* (London: Catholic
     Truth Society, 1907), 113–14.

116 Vladimir Guettée, *The Papacy: Its Historic Origin and Primitive Relations with
     the Eastern Churches* (New York, NY: Minos, 1866), 95–96.

117 In, *Nicene and Post-Nicene Fathers: A Select Library of the Christian Church*,
     vol. 14, 15.

118 Dvornik, *Byzantium and the Roman Primacy*, 33.

119 Ibid., 32.

120 Siecienski, *The Papacy and the Orthodox: Sources and History of a Debate*, 153.

121 Meyendorff, *Orthodoxy and Catholicity*, 54.

122 Guettée, *The Papacy: Its Historic Origin and Primitive Relations with the Eastern
     Churches*, 41.

123 Michael Whelton, *Two Paths: Papal Monarchy, Collegial Tradition* (Salisbury,

MA: Regina Orthodox Press, 1998), 37–38.

124 Karlo Broussard, *Meeting the Protestant Response: How to Answer Common Comebacks to Catholic Arguments* (El Cajon, CA: Catholic Answers Press, 2022), 73–82.

125 Siecienski, *The Papacy and the Orthodox: Sources and History of a Debate*, 141.

126 Chapman, *The Condemnation of Pope Honorius*, 71.

127 Price and Graumann, *The Council of Ephesus of 431: Documents and Proceedings*, 364–66.

128 See session 2, in Richard Price and Michael Gaddis, *The Acts of the Council of Chalcedon*, vol. 2 (Liverpool: Liverpool University Press, 2005), 24.

129 E. Giles, *Documents Illustrating Papal Authority: A.D. 96-454* (London: S.P.C.K, 1952), 328.

130 Ibid., 330.

131 Ibid., 322.

132 Schmemann, *The Historical Road of Eastern Orthodoxy*, 241.

133 Siecienski, *The Papacy and the Orthodox: Sources and History of a Debate*, 142.

134 Chadwick, *East and West: The Making of a Rift in the Church: From Apostolic Times until the Council of Florence*, 100.

135 Eusebius, *Eusebius' Ecclesiastical History*, trans. Christian Frederic Crusé (Peabody, MA: Hendrickson, 2009), 183.

136 See James McCue, "The Roman Primacy in the Second Century and the Problem of the Development of Dogma," *Theological Studies* 25 (1964): 161–96, as cited in Siecienski, *The Papacy and the Orthodox: Sources and History of a Debate*, 148–49.

137 Eusebius, *Eusebius' Ecclesiastical History*, 183.

138 Giles, *Documents Illustrating Papal Authority: A.D. 96-454*, 131.

139 See Denzinger 232, in Hünermann et al., *Compendium of Creeds, Definitions, and Declarations on Matters of Faith and Morals*, 86.

140 See Denzinger 233, in Hünermann et al., *Compendium of Creeds, Definitions, and Declarations on Matters of Faith and Morals*, 86.

141 See Denzinger 235, in Hünermann et al., *Compendium of Creeds, Definitions, and Declarations on Matters of Faith and Morals*, 86.

142 Siecienski, *The Papacy and the Orthodox: Sources and History of a Debate*, 184.

143 J.N.D. Kelly, *The Oxford Dictionary of Popes* (Oxford: Oxford University Press, 1991), 51.

144 Footnote 2 in Chadwick, *East and West: The Making of a Rift in the Church:*

From Apostolic Times until the Council of Florence, 83.

145 Chadwick, *East and West: The Making of a Rift in the Church: From Apostolic Times until the Council of Florence*, 210–11.

146 Gregory the Great, *Registrum Epistolarum,* 7.33, in *Nicene and Post-Nicene Fathers: A Select Library of the Christian Church*, vol. 12, 226.

147 Gregory the Great, *Registrum Epistolarum,* 9.68, in *Nicene and Post-Nicene Fathers: A Select Library of the Christian Church*, ed. Philip Schaff and Henry Wace, vol. 13 (Peabody, MA: Hendrickson, 2004), 19.

148 Tanner, *Decrees of the Ecumenical Councils, Volume 2: Trent to Vatican II*, 814.

149 Gregory the Great, *Registrum Epistolarum* 9.59, in *Nicene and Post-Nicene Fathers: A Select Library of the Christian Church*, vol. 13, 15.

150 Siecienski, *The Papacy and the Orthodox: Sources and History of a Debate*, 192.

151 Ibid., 193.

152 Philip Schaff, *History of the Christian Church,* vol. 4 (Grand Rapids, MI: Eerdmans, 1908), 224.

153 Gregory the Great, *Registrum Epistolarum*, 5.43, in *Nicene and Post-Nicene Fathers: A Select Library of the Christian Church*, vol. 12, 178.

154 Meyendorff, *Orthodoxy and Catholicity*, 27.

155 See chap. 1 in Dvornik, *Byzantium and the Roman Primacy.*

156 See Siecienski, *The Papacy and the Orthodox: Sources and History of a Debate*, 156.

157 Meyendorff, *Orthodoxy and Catholicity*, 27.

158 Siecienski, *The Papacy and the Orthodox: Sources and History of a Debate*, 156.

159 Giles, *Documents Illustrating Papal Authority: A.D. 96-454*, 131.

160 Extracts from the Acts, in *Nicene and Post-Nicene Fathers: A Select Library of the Christian Church*, vol. 14, 223.

161 See Leo, *Sermo*, 5 in Giles, *Documents Illustrating Papal Authority: A.D. 96-454*, 281–82.

162 Ayer, *A Source Book for Ancient Church History: From the Apostolic Age to the Close of the Conciliar Period*, 536.

163 Cleenewerck, *His Broken Body: Understanding and Healing the Schism Between the Roman Catholic and Eastern Orthodox Churches*, 214.

164 See Siecienski, *The Papacy and the Orthodox: Sources and History of a Debate*, 183.

165 Price and Gaddis, *The Acts of the Council of Chalcedon*, vol. 1, 10.

166 Maximus the Confessor, *Opuscula theologica et polemica*, 12, PG 91, 141–46; English translation in Metropolitan Hilarion Alfeyev, *Orthodox Christianity,* vol. 1, trans. Basil Bush (Crestwood, NY: St. Vladimir's Seminary Press,

2011), 110, as quoted in Siecienski, *The Papacy and the Orthodox: Sources and History of a Debate*, 202.

167 Mansi, x, 677–78, in Chapman, *The Condemnation of Pope Honorius*, 27.

168 Price, *The Acts of the Second Council of Nicaea (787)*, 156–58.

169 Ibid.

170 See footnote 44 in Price, *The Acts of the Second Council of Nicaea (787)*, 155.

171 See footnote 86 in Siecienski, *The Papacy and the Orthodox: Sources and History of a Debate*, 213.

172 Guettée, *The Papacy: Its Historic Origin and Primitive Relations with the Eastern Churches*, 264.

173 Siecienski, *The Papacy and the Orthodox: Sources and History of a Debate*, 187.

174 Ibid., 223.

175 Tanner, *Decrees of the Ecumenical Councils, Volume 1: Nicaea I—Lateran V*, 236.

176 The Letter of Pope Agatho, in *Nicene and Post-Nicene Fathers: A Select Library of the Christian Church*, vol. 14, 331–32.

177 See Erickson, *The Challenge of Our Past: Studies in Orthodox Canon Law and Church History*, 74.

178 Mansi, x, 806, quoted in T.W. Allies, *The See of St. Peter: The Rock of the Church, the Source of Jurisdiction, and the Centre of Unity* (London: Burns & Lambert, 1850), 120.

179 Price and Booth, *The Acts of the Lateran Synod of 649*, 148.

180 Mansi, x, 913, quoted in Allies, *The See of St. Peter: The Rock of the Church, the Source of Jurisdiction, and the Centre of Unity*, 124–25.

181 Gregory the Great, *Registrum Epistolarum*, 7.40, in *Nicene and Post-Nicene Fathers: A Select Library of the Christian Church*, vol. 12, 229.

182 Guettée, *The Papacy: Its Historic Origin and Primitive Relations with the Eastern Churches*, 228.

183 John Chapman, *Bishop Gore and the Catholic Claims* (London: Longmans, Green, and Co., 1905), 84.

184 Gregory the Great, *Registrum Epistolarum*, 9,59, in *Nicene and Post-Nicene Fathers: A Select Library of the Christian Church*, vol. 13, 15.

185 Price and Graumann, *The Council of Ephesus of 431: Documents and Proceedings*, 131.

186 Gregory the Great, *Registrum Epistolarum,* 9.68, in *Nicene and Post-Nicene Fathers: A Select Library of the Christian Church*, vol. 13, 19.

187 Price and Gaddis, *The Acts of the Council of Chalcedon*, vol. 2, 70.

188 Damick, *Orthodoxy and Heterodoxy: Finding the Way to Christ in a Complicated Religious Landscape*, 68.

189 George Dion. Dragas, "The 8th Ecumenical Council: Constantinople IV (879/880) and the Condemnation of the Filioque Addition and Doctrine," Orthodox Outlet for Dogmatic Enquiries, December 28, 2009, accessed October 13, 2022, http://www.oodegr.com/english/dogma/synodoi/8th_Synod_Dragas.htm.

190 Gill, *The Council of Florence*, 145.

191 Ibid., 149.

192 Price and Graumann, *The Council of Ephesus of 431: Documents and Proceedings*, 469.

193 Gill, *The Council of Florence*, 149.

194 For the creed read out and accepted by the council fathers at Ephesus, see Price and Graumann, *The Council of Ephesus of 431: Documents and Proceedings*, 447.

195 Ibid.

196 Siecienski, *The Filioque: History of a Doctrinal Controversy*, 65.

197 Ott, *Fundamentals of Catholic Dogma*, 442.

198 Ibid.

199 Damick, *Orthodoxy and Heterodoxy: Finding the Way to Christ in a Complicated Religious Landscape*, 91–92.

200 See the entry under "Art" in John Anthony McGuckin, *The Westminster Handbook to Patristic Theology* (Louisville, KY: Westminster John Knox Press, 2006), 32.

201 Louth, "Is Development of Doctrine a Valid Category for Orthodox Theology?," 47.

202 Cleenewerck, *His Broken Body: Understanding and Healing the Schism Between the Roman Catholic and Eastern Orthodox Churches*, 43.

203 Dennis Bratcher, ed., "The Confession of Dositheus (Eastern Orthodox, 1672)," http://www.crivoice.org/creeddositheus.html.

204 Diocese of Phoenix, "The Restored Order of Sacraments of Initiation," EWTN, accessed October 12, 2022, https://www.ewtn.com/catholicism/library/restored-order-of-sacraments-of-initiation--3808.

205 Lawrence Feingold, *Touched by Christ: The Sacramental Economy* (Steubenville, OH: Emmaus Academic, 2021), 140.

206 *Didache*, 7, quoted in J.B. Lightfoot and J.R. Harmer, *The Apostolic Fathers:*

Revised Greek Texts with Introductions and English Translations (Grand Rapids, MI: Baker Book House, 1988), 232.

207 See Feingold, Touched by Christ: The Sacramental Economy, 209–10.

208 Ibid., 210.

209 De Indis et de Iure Belli Relectiones, ed. E. Nys, trans. J.P. Bates, Classics of International Law (Washington: 1917), 142, as quoted in Francis A. Sullivan, Salvation Outside the Church: Tracing the History of the Catholic Response (Eugene, OR: Wipf & Stock, 2002), 72.

210 Congregation for the Doctrine of the Faith, "Letter to the Archbishop of Boston," EWTN, August 8, 1949, accessed October 13, 2022, https://www.ewtn.com/catholicism/library/letter-to-the-archbishop-of-boston-2076.

211 See Anthologion, vol. 2 (Rome: Sacred Oriental Congregation, 1974), 1607–16.

212 See the Letter of the Holy Father Francis to the Bishops of the Whole World, That Accompanies the Apostolic Letter Motu Proprio Traditionis Custodes.

213 Jaroslav Pelikan, The Christian Tradition: A History of the Development of Doctrine, Volume 2: The Spirit of Eastern Christendom, 600-1700 (Chicago: University of Chicago Press, 1974), 177.

214 Andrew Louth, Greek East and Latin West: The Church AD 681-1071 (Crestwood, NY: St. Vladimirs Seminary Press, 2007), 307.

215 Pelikan, The Christian Tradition: A History of the Development of Doctrine, Volume 2: The Spirit of Eastern Christendom, 600-1700, 177.

216 Chadwick, East and West: The Making of a Rift in the Church: From Apostolic Times until the Council of Florence, 201.

217 Rick Brannan, ed., Lexham Research Lexicon of the Greek New Testament, Lexham Research Lexicons (Bellingham, WA: Lexham Press, 2020).

218 Joachim Jeremias, The Eucharistic Words of Jesus, trans. Norman Perrin (London: SCM Press, 1987), 63–64.